FOR

Tony Sutherland is a rare breed of minister. He is a low maintenance, high impact member of our leadership team at Free Chapel. Tony came to us ten years ago at a time when we were in major transition and fervently praying and searching for strong leadership in the area of worship. His insight and experience served us greatly in those formative years of change and expansion. After offering him the main worship position here he felt led to be used of God in more of a volunteer capacity without expectation of pay or reimbursement, while continuing his itinerate ministry. We supported him then and we continue to support him now.

About a year later, God began to speak to Tony about taking the baton as a Children's worship leader here on staff. My heart was greatly encouraged by this. Therefore, after several key meetings and prayer as a staff, we asked him to come on board to oversee, develop and nurture the worship experience of our kids. We knew he was obviously anointed and fully equipped to assume higher levels of leadership, but his heart burned with an eager desire to ignite a flame of worship in the heart of the next generation. Tony graciously accepted this assignment and almost immediately we began to witness a powerful transformation in the worship expression of our children!

I don't know many worship leaders and ministers with his abilities who are content to lead kids' worship. It touches my heart every time I think of him blessing our kids with his fabulous talent. We are also privileged to have him regularly lead worship here for various other main and special events. What a songwriter, what a worship leader, what a servant!

Part of our mission here is also to empower and equip other churches around the world. Tony is helping fulfill this part of our vision. We would be amiss to ignore this calling on his life, and so we are proud to support and release him. Thus, Tony continues to travel abroad, using his exceptional gifts of evangelism, teaching, preaching, writing and worship leading to serve other pastors and churches. However, he is always faithful to prioritize his responsibilities here no matter where in the world His ministry carries him.

Tony's maturity in the Word of God is without exception. This book is a powerful extension of his loyalty towards me, my family, and our leaders here at Free Chapel. Anointing, integrity, sincerity, and leadership: all from someone who has the heart of a servant and fully knows his place in the Body of Christ. My family and I are forever grateful that Tony has written **Covered** specifically to raise up people to pray for us. I know pastors everywhere will be greatly encouraged by it as well. Get it, read it, and put it into *forward* motion!

Jentezen Franklin
Senior Pastor — Free Chapel
Kingdom Connection Ministries
Gainesville, GA

ENDORSEMENTS

Tony Sutherland has been a long time member and worship leader here at Free Chapel. His servant heart is without question and is a loyal supporter of our pastoral staff. His life and ministry are a true reflection of one who believes in fervent and dedicated prayer for those in spiritual authority. We are continually stressing the critical importance for our congregation to sincerely pray for our pastor, his wife and their family on a consistent basis. Tony powerfully and profoundly defines the call and role of the intercessor and provides detailed and practical insight to effectively pray for pastors and key leaders. **Covered** *is a MUST for seasoned prayer warriors as well as newly forming prayer ministries in the local church. After reading this book, your prayer life and support for your leaders will be reignited and realigned.*

Tracy Page
Executive Pastor — Free Chapel
Gainesville, GA

Without question, **Covered** *is a key resource for ministry leaders who are committed to excellence and lasting impact in God's kingdom. Trends, strategies and tactics have come and gone in every generation, but the felt impact of intercession on a leader's life will produce lasting and powerful results! Tony Sutherland has clearly outlined a strategic offensive game plan for every church and para-church leader; all this from a man who truly lives out what he is preaching. I know,* my life and ministry have felt the direct impact of Tony's faith and prayers.

Jon Bennett, M.Th
Pastor & Leadership Coach
Alpharetta, GA

In **Covered**, Tony Sutherland eloquently and passionately conveys the heart of a true intercessor while also poignantly identifying the deep, heart-needs of the leader. As he so adequately points out, no spiritual leader is without the need for a firmly established and constant covering of prayer. Tony powerfully articulates the leader's regular struggles and his absolute necessity for devoted intercessors. As a Pastor, I fully recognize my own need for a surrounding of love, support and consistent prayer for my family and ministry. Tony, not only expresses in concept what effective prayer looks like, but also presents a detailed and practical plan to intentionally pray for leaders. I highly recommend this insightful book as a guide to any pastor, intercessor or prayer team desiring to seriously understand their role and take their intercessory prayer ministries to the next level.

Danny Chambers
Senior Pastor — Oasis Church
Nashville, TN

If we truly believe prayer changes things, then churches and ministry leaders will be greatly impacted by **Covered**. This book is personal, practical, and powerful. Tony says things leaders want to say, but often can't. This book not only calls us to pray for leaders; but also to truly intercede for them specifically, consistently, and effectively. I'll be sure this book gets into the hands of our staff, volunteers, prayer partners and our entire church family.

Dave Divine
Lead Pastor — The Church at Chapelhill
Douglasville, GA

I admire Tony Sutherland for his many talents but more importantly, his anointing in songwriting and ministry in leading worship. I have worked with Tony in many capacities and found him to be extremely insightful, creative and passionately dedicated to his calling. **Covered** will minister to you about one of the most important subjects known to all believers... prayer... particularly that of faithfully praying for your spiritual leaders. As you apply these principles to your life, not only will you experience new growth and greater maturity, but your leaders will also powerfully benefit from the labor of your prayers.

Richie Hughes
Author — "Start Here, Go Anywhere"
www.richiehughes.com

As a couple dedicated to pursuing God's call on our lives, we have experienced not only the triumphs of ministry, but also the trials. However, a major key to our longevity in marriage and ministry these many years is knowing we have had the right people beside us every step of the way who were truly praying for us. COVERED exposes the real life struggles that today's pastors face and gives us all a powerful wake up call to action! We can be the solution instead of the problem. Our spiritual leaders need us now more than ever before. There is no greater way to lift the hearts and hands of ministers than to pray for them. My prayer is that as you read this book that God will awaken a heartfelt desire within you to cover your leaders!

Sherri Sutherland
Tony's Wife of 25 Years
Atlanta, GA

ACKNOWLEDGEMENTS

I am continually grateful for my amazing wife Sherri who unceasingly and fervently prays for me. None rivals her unwavering loyalty. I would be nothing without her unconditional love, constant encouragement, sensitivity and honesty. Her discernment has been critical throughout my life and ministry. I heavily depend on her to hear from God and her boldness to speak the truth in love.

Thanks to my mother Glenda, who is a source of great inspiration and has been a loyal and faithful prayer warrior for me my whole life. I cannot tell you the number of times when spiritual opposition, anxiety, and uncertainty has gripped me prior to ministry moments. Yet, her love, advice and prayers have brought instant comfort, quickened my repose and enabled me to flow in Holy Ghost power. Her own intercession, coupled with the coordinating of other mighty and seasoned prayer warriors, has reaped an abundant harvest in my ministry.

My deep appreciation also goes out to all the pastors, leaders and great men of God who read this manuscript and offered their generous endorsements. I am grateful for their insight and wisdom along the way and deeply appreciate and value their influence in my life and ministry. Thanks also for the grand opportunity to be a part of what God has done through your lives and ministries.

Of course I will always be indebted to my Grandma Sutherland. Her life proved that our prayers last long beyond our days here on earth. Her prayers still carry eternal weight and immeasurable influence that have ultimately touched nations through my ministry. The lives I am impacting today all began in a red swivel chair where she faithfully and tearfully cried out to God for me every day of her life while she was living. I am a powerful product of her intercession.

A heartfelt thanks goes to my great friend and fellow Grace preacher, Pastor Aaron Davis (AKA The Tattoo Preacher) who offered insight and important editorial information to this work. His heart to touch the untouchable and reach the unreachable inspires me.

I am truly grateful for Pastors Jentezen Franklin, Tracy Page and the staff and leadership of Free Chapel. It is an honor to minister along side all of you and be part of what God is doing through this phenomenal ministry.

To my loyal friends who make up the Worldwide Intercessors Network (W.I.N.), I am truly thankful for you. My family and I are living proof of your decision and dedication to intercede for us. Your prayers have helped to open incredible doors and pushed the opposition out of the way as we ran through them. Together we W.I.N.!

TONY SUTHERLAND

COVERED

Praying for your
Spiritual Leaders

COVERED

Praying for your
Spiritual Leaders

Tony Sutherland Ministries, Inc.
508 Westwind Way
Ball Ground, GA 30107
www.tonysutherland.com

Cover Design by Michael Hamilton. www.mchcreative.com

CONTENTS

INTRODUCTION

"The most powerful weapon on earth is the human soul on fire." ~ **Ferdinand Foch**

Several years ago, just prior to launching my full time itinerate ministry, I was invited to minister at a pastor's conference in Evansville, Indiana. I was to lead worship for the morning session and share the vision of my ministry with a group of pastors at a leadership luncheon later that afternoon. However, there was one catch. I had just resigned from a worship pastorate at a church in Atlanta, Georgia and was in the throes of a major life transition trying to figure out what God wanted me to do next. I knew I loved Jesus and that I was passionate for a move of the Holy Spirit in my life and among God's people. I was confident in my knowledge of the Word of God and in my abilities as a worship leader. I could also speak and minister effectively under the anointing. However, the last thing I was prepared to do was share my ministry vision. I needed more time to prepare my thoughts. I still had so many questions: Why did God throw me into this situation unscripted? How could I muster the gumption to stand in front of all these pastors and speak with any shred of authority? What would I say to them? It was obvious God had me right where He wanted me.

"Do not worry about how or what you are to say; for it will be given you in that hour what you are to say. For it is not you who speak, but it is the Spirit of your Father who speaks in you." ~ **Matthew 10:19 NASB**

On the night before the conference, while I was lying on my bed wide-awake prayerfully pondering what I was to say to these pastors, the Holy Spirit breathed the word "PILOT" into my spirit. In that moment, I could see the pilot light of a stove burning and from this vision God spoke His intentions of the scope of what my ministry would eventually evolve into. For the next several minutes as I lay there in the dark listening to God and watching pictures race through my mind, God began to unveil His awesome plan for my life. I was about to be catapulted by the Holy Spirit into a ministry that would help to ignite a passion for God's presence in the hearts of people all around the world. That night God ignited my heart with a thousand fires of HIS passion!

"When you set yourself on fire, people love to come and see you burn." ~ **John Wesley**

From that 'one word' I leapt out of bed and under the inspiration of the Holy Spirit began to write out an acronym of what would eventually become the mission of my ministry. To this very day my ministry continues to equip and empower the worshipping church culture through the following five areas: Pastoral Consultation, Intercession, Live Worship Online Resources and Teaching & Training (P.I.L.O.T.). That next day at the conference I boldly stood in front of those pastors and shared the heartbeat of my ministry as if I had been doing it for years (When God gives you a word be assured that He will perform it). In the years that have followed that profound season, God has continued to use me to release a passion for His presence, freedom for worship, deposit seeds for renewal & revival and declare the uncompromised New Covenant gospel of Grace to hundreds of thousands of people in numerous congregations across the country and around the world. I have received scores of emails, Internet posts and phone calls from leaders whose churches have been encouraged, affirmed and forever changed through my ministry encounters. I have also been afforded the great privilege to provide valuable leadership training and mentorship to the next generation of leaders and have helped to facilitate freedom, renewal and growth in hundreds of churches. To this I give God all the glory!

The ongoing vision of my ministry is to be the catalyst for a mighty Grace awakening and a worship revival around the world. It is my strong belief that these two things will stir a powerful desperation in the hearts of people for a move of the Holy Spirit to invade their individual lives, homes, churches, cities and nations. My heart burns for people to return to the priority of God's presence and to give the gospel of Grace preeminence in the church. Thus, I have dedicated my life to inspire and challenge the church to embrace an end time move of the Holy Spirit and the gospel of Grace. Thus doing, the flame of their passion for Jesus will never smolder out! We will set the church on fire when we point more to what Jesus has done than what we should be doing.

"The burnt offering itself shall remain on the hearth on the altar all night until the morning, and the fire on the altar is to be kept burning on it... The fire on the altar shall be kept burning on it. It shall not go out... Fire shall be kept burning continually on the altar; it is not to go out. ~ **Leviticus 6:9-13 NASB**

All of this leads to the reason for this book... In the early days of my newly forming ministry I began to sense the urgency for strong prayer support if I were to survive the challenges that awaited me. This led me to the duty of commissioning a network of intercessors for what God had called me to. At first I tried to interest others to take the charge due to the enormity of the undertaking because I felt I had "more important" obligations to focus on than raising up dedicated prayer partners. It sounds ridiculous now, but at the time I actually believed there were other more important areas I needed to give my attention than developing a prayer network. I already have a strong personal prayer life so I thought that I could delegate this responsibility to someone else. I even asked one of my most trustworthy friends and prayer supporters to accept the assignment. However, the more that I shunned the responsibility for developing a personal prayer team, the more the urgency brewed within my own heart. Eventually, after I had exhausted all my efforts to hand it over to someone else, I sensed from the Holy Spirit that it was my job and not someone else's. In that instant I realized I could no longer delegate the responsibility of raising up intercessors to others! I realized that prayer is the FIRST priority of my ministry and everything else I do is a result from the abundance or the lack thereof. There is no greater work of ministry than the administration of prayer.

"Prayer does not fit us for the greater work. Prayer is the greater work." ~ **Oswald Chambers**

That moment was a major turning point for me and as I look back I feel very fortunate for it to have happened in the early stages of my ministry. Thus, I immediately began to enlist a group of trusted and dedicated prayer partners comprised mostly of relatives, seasoned saints faithful to prayer, close friends, strong acquaintances and all those whom I knew had been praying for me for many years. To this day I continue to send them prayer updates through emails, phone calls and text messages. In these updates I regularly alert them of special considerations for prayer in every area of my life (I.e. family, finances, health issues, travel schedule, ministry concerns, etc.)

Eventually, I gave my prayer network a special name: Worldwide Intercessors Network — *"Together we W.I.N.!"* Sometime later I developed a pamphlet containing several topical prayers to better inform, inspire and guide our intercessors (I share these on pages 90-103). That early intercessor's guide eventually evolved into the book you are now reading. I cannot tell you the countless times when I have sensed the immediacy for others to pray for me regarding critical situations directly linked to my family, ministry and personal life. During these times I have been able to lean heavily upon my trustworthy intercessors for support. Whenever I experience spiritual oppression, sickness, financial strain, family crisis, ministry hindrances, personnel conflict and more, I can rely on my top prayer partners to link arms with me in fervent intercession. I tell you the truth; because of the dedication of my intercessors I have experienced the overcoming power of God as it flows through me and around me. When satan comes to harass me I know my prayer team is nearby and I can count on them day or night to pray.

The book you now hold in your hands is a powerful prayer tool that comes from a passionate devotion to the process of raising up a network of intercessors for my ministry. I offer it those of you who are answering the clarion call of God to help develop your prayer team and equip prayer partners for spiritual warfare on behalf of your pastors and leaders. This book will also powerfully serve as a valuable resource for pastors as they develop their personal prayer team and other intercessory teams within their local churches and various ministries.

I strongly encourage you to carefully study this book and refer back to it often during times of intercessory prayer. It will be tremendous ammunition for your prayer arsenal. My prayer for you is that as you pour over these pages the Holy Spirit will awaken a hunger within you to mightily intercede for those who are faithful to the call of God to watch over you and instruct you in the ways of His Kingdom. May the Lord grant you strength, discernment, authority and breakthrough power as you intercede on behalf of your leaders and their call to lay down their lives for the sake of the Gospel of Jesus Christ.

Chapter 1

UNCOVERING THE FACTS

"You have left your first love." ~ **Exodus 28:42 NKJV**

Before we get to the critical subject of covering our spiritual leaders through prayer, we must *uncover* the facts. When we pull the veil back from modern day ministry, we discover than an alarming number of ministers in the body of Christ today are deeply troubled, suffering burnout and eventually dropping out of the ministry all together. According to *Sunscape Ministries* of Colorado, which serves clergy in crises, approximately 1,600 pastors per month are terminated or forced to resign their pulpit due to moral failure, burnout, or contention in their churches. According to Francis A. Schaeffer Institute of Church Leadership Development, after years of researching pastoral trends they have found that ministers are in a very dangerous occupation! They are perhaps the single most stressed and frustrated working professionals, even more than doctors, lawyers or politicians. CNNMoney.com recently published an article entitled *Stressful Jobs That Pay Badly*. Among this list of jobs was *Music Ministry Director* at a moderate number 5 and *Minister* at 10. On a side note, I found it interesting that music directors by and large are paid more than Pastors. Another startling find in a study conducted by psychologist Richard Blackmon (with ties to Fuller Seminary and Dr. Archibald Heart) reported that the average insurance costs to churches for dealing with mental breakdowns among clergy is four percent higher than ANY secular industry.

Pastoral burnout is of vital concern to the body of Christ. Too many of our key leaders feel vocationally exhausted, completely depleted of energy and spiritual vitality and lack the resources to fulfill their call. The good news is that pastoral burnout can be faced honestly and remedial action can be taken. However, for too many ministers, burnout is like an unattended disease or even a hidden cancer. When truthfully faced and admitted, pastors can find healing from their battle wounds. When hidden, burnout becomes a form of acedia that manifests itself in isolation, insulation and evasion. Acedia is one of the classic *Seven Deadly Sins* first outlined by the desert fathers (early monastic founders living in the deserts of Egypt in the fourth century). Acedia is truly deadly for ministers. It kills the God-given dreams and aspirations of a God-called man. It is a kind of spiritual lethargy, apathy, hopelessness and an *"I-just-don't-care-anymore"* condition. The sad truth for the majority of ministers today is that they just don't care anymore. Ironically, what leads a pastor to apathy, depression, fatigue and sin is the temptation to ignore his own spiritual emptiness by becoming as busy as possible. A pastor appearing unscathed is many times nothing more than a great cover up of his own shame, failure and inadequacy. Before a minister knows what is gradually happening, burnout ambushes him by *surprise.* Let's look at just a few of the alarming statistics.

The Stats

The following statistics and percentages reflect current and accurate averages based on general consensus from numerous cites referenced in the Endnotes.

50% of pastors say they need to take a leave of absence from ministry due to depression and discouragement.

70% of pastors constantly fight depression. Nearly the same percent admits to having a lower self-esteem now than when they started out in ministry.

90% of pastors feel inadequate to cope with ministry demands.

Nearly 80% of pastors and their wives are completely discouraged. Almost 70% say they have no close friends.

The typical pastor has his greatest impact at a church in years 5 through years 14 of his pastorate. Unfortunately, the average pastor lasts only five years at a church.

80% of seminary students will leave the ministry within the first five years. 70% will leave the ministry after 10 years and over 60% have been fired twice.

40% of pastors say they have considered leaving their pastorates in the last three months.

57% of pastors would leave the ministry if they had another viable financial option. 58% of their wives work outside the home because the family needs the income.

80% of pastors' wives wish their husband would choose another profession.

80% of pastors admit that ministry negatively affects their families admitting that they have little to no time with their wives.

Nearly 50% of pastors say ministry is hazardous to their family's well-being.

On a scale from 1-10, pastors overall rate their family's health as a 4.

Approximately 80% of pastors say they do not have a good marriage.

Almost 60% of pastors' marriages will end in divorce. Nearly 40% have already ended in divorce.

45% of pastors' wives say the greatest danger to their family is physical, emotional, mental and spiritual burnout.

The majority of pastors' wives admit that the most destructive event that occurred in their marriage and family was the day they entered the ministry.

Almost 40% of pastors currently struggle with some form of sexual sin and 20% regularly deal with sexual misconduct.

Over 50% of pastors struggle with Internet pornography.

33% of pastors confess to inappropriate sexual behavior and indiscretions with someone in the church. 40% admit to having had a full-blown affair. This does not include the sad number of their wives who have also had affairs.

These statistics are heart wrenching! That is why I have written this book. I want to do my part in helping put a stop to these atrocities. In serving as a worship leader for many years, I have developed a sincere fondness and a deep burden to serve and encourage pastors (See 2 Kings 3:11). This is primarily a book about GIVING GRACE to our leaders and in this great and final hour of the church, our pastors need Grace now more than ever before. Yes, there are precautions ministers themselves can take to prevent the plight of burnout and dropout. However, instead of pointing all the blame towards them for their demise, we should love them, fervently pray for them and seek ways to reach out and restore them. Many times, rather than focus on what WE can do to help these weary, wounded soldiers, we tend to judge them from our lofty towers of self-righteousness. All too often, rather than *pray* for our leaders, we *prey* on them, attacking them for their inconsistencies, inabilities and uncertainties. This only further attributes to the increase in statistics like the ones listed above. The truth is, praying for our spiritual leaders has never been more crucial. Far too many pastors feel completely isolated and exposed to the onslaught of demonic aggravation as they stand in the battlefield for the souls of men.

3 Reasons Pastors Fall

It is my deep personal conviction that pastors fall and ultimately sabotage their influence for the following three reasons: ACCEPTING DISCOURAGEMENT (Numbers 32:9; Ezra 4:4; Nehemiah 6:9), LACK OF PRAYER COVERING (Mark 14:38) and perhaps the greatest single reason a pastor falls is SELF-SUSTAINING PRIDE (Proverbs 16:18, Revelation 1:20-2:5). This is when a pastor no longer relies on God's Grace and loses sight of his first love.

"As for the mystery of the seven stars which you saw in My right hand, and the seven golden lampstands: the seven stars are the angels of the seven churches and the seven lampstands are the seven churches. To the angel of the church in Ephesus write: The One who holds the seven stars in His right hand, the One who walks among the seven golden lampstands, says this: "I know your deeds and your toil and perseverance, and that you cannot tolerate evil men, and you put to the test those who call themselves apostles, and they are not, and you found them to be false; and you have perseverance and have endured for My name's sake, and have not grown weary. But I have this against you, that you have left your first love.

26

Therefore remember from where you have fallen, and repent and do the deeds you did at first; or else I am coming to you and will remove your lampstand out of its place—unless you repent." ~ **Revelation 1:20-2:5 NASB**

At first glance this passage is shrouded in imagery and mystery (as much of Revelation is). However, when you look a little closer you can clearly see that God is dealing with a fallen pastor. Notice carefully the usage of symbolism here.

"As for the mystery of the seven STARS which you saw IN MY RIGHT HAND... the seven STARS are the ANGELS of the seven churches." ~ **Revelation 1:20 NASB**

It is interesting that pastors are referred to as *"angels"* or shining *"stars"* signifying they are very special in God's eyes and holds them securely in His right hand (symbolic of favor). This is of significant encouragement to spiritual leaders everywhere, especially to those who are struggling. Each "lampstand" (menorah) symbolizes the seven churches. Although the pastor of the church at Ephesus had lost sight of God's Grace and had fallen from his first love, God confirms that He is still holding him in His right hand. It does not say that God cast the pastor out of fellowship with Him. However, it does say that He would remove the LAMPSTAND (the pastor's church) unless he repented (changed his mindset) and returned to His first love. So often pastors attempt to sustain the ministry on THEIR LOVE for God instead of HIS LOVE for them. Ministers must repent of the prideful self-sustaining mindset. All too often, pastors get caught up in the cycle of (1) keeping THEIR commitment to God and the people and (2) maintaining THEIR passion for Him, instead of relying on HIS LOVE and commitment to sustain them. The beautiful paradox of the New Covenant is that Christ GAVE His life for us and yet KEEPS His love for us! Jesus is our FIRST true LOVE!

"This is love, not that we loved God, BUT THAT HE LOVED US..." ~ **1 John 4:10**

Here, Jesus redefines the standard of love and service. This is vitally important for ministers to grasp. It is not that we love God but that He FIRST LOVES us. The demand of the Old Covenant pattern was to love the Lord Your God with all your heart, soul and strength (Deuteronomy 11). Pastors get caught in the demanding trap of the Old Covenant standard: to love God with all THEIR strength and to serve Him with THEIR whole heart. To this they eventually find themselves broke down on the side of the road of ministry with no desire to continue. Ministry is not based on more numbers, better results, capital campaigns, souls saved, buildings built, sermons preached, books written, programs implemented and the like. Ministers are sustained through an ongoing vital relationship with Jesus Christ founded on what He has done for them, not what they do for Him. When pastors lose sight of this it could mean the beginning of the end for their ministry.

The *removing of the lampstand* in Revelation 2:5 has been traditionally taught as God removing His Spirit from pastor's lives and churches when they fall. This is not in context with the passage. The removal of the lampstand directly refers to a pastor LOSING HIS CHURCH. *"The seven lampstands ARE THE SEVEN CHURCHES* (Revelation 1:20). When a pastor falls he may possibly forfeit his influence and right to lead. Although the sheep may scatter to find other pastures, God still holds the pastor in His hand. The pastor at Ephesus obviously did not fail in his efforts to perform great works.

"I know your deeds and your toil and perseverance, and that you cannot tolerate evil men, and you put to the test those who call themselves apostles, and they are not, and you found them to be false; and you have perseverance and have endured for My name's sake, and have not grown weary." ~
Revelation 2:2-3 NASB

Here God wasn't condemning the pastor for failing but rather COMMENDING him for a job well done. However, God immediately gets to the heart of the matter.

"I have this against you, that you have left your first love."
~ Revelation 2:4 NASB

We must know God's heart to better understand His words when He says, *"I have this against you."* God is never against us in a derogatory way. The scriptures say, *"If God be FOR US, who can be against us."* (Romans 8:31). And in another passage just before that, *"There is therefore now NO CONDEMNATION to those in Christ Jesus."* (Romans 8:1) This includes ministers. God never condemns us and is ALWAYS for us. However, God is opposed to self-sustaining pride not because of what it does to Him, but because of what it does to

29

ministers. His heart is especially inclined towards pastors when they are deviating from their purpose. This is because God doesn't want anything to prevent them from fulfilling their destiny.

Although God was pleased with this pastor's efforts, He gave a loving rebuke and compassionate warning that unless he quickly made a U-turn back towards an intimate relationship with Him, his ministry was headed towards disaster. Note that the pastor hadn't fallen from his place of ministry but rather the PRIORITY of ministry! He wasn't failing at ministry by any means. Rather, he was failing to prioritize God's love and finished work, and instead basing his ministry on self-efforts. This clearly warrants strong caution for ministers. Ministers succeed in life and ministry when they regularly admit they need an abundance of Grace for every situation and willfully receive it (Romans 5:17). Ministers are not by any means exempt from Grace. The moment ministers think themselves entitled because of their faithfulness, experience, skills, labor, performance, connections, accomplishments, etc. they set themselves up for failure! Through Grace, God sets up spiritual leaders for TOTAL success.

The previous appalling statistics reveal that it can be potentially devastating when we try to hold up the ministry in our own strength and much service. This story of Uzzah the priest in 2 Samuel 6:3-8 gives us powerful insight into this tragedy. When Uzzah attempted to reach out and catch the falling ark as it tumbled from the ox cart, the results were fatal. Likewise, the weight of the ministry can literally consume and crush us when we try to hold it up in our own strength. And the sad irony is we end up losing the very thing we strive to maintain.

Once again, it is critical to understand that when ministers fall (regardless of the reasons or circumstances surrounding their dilemma) it is not up to us to judge them but to fervently love and pray for them. We must trust God's love and sovereignty. He still has a destiny for His chosen vessels. If God put the stars in their place He can surely put fallen pastors (stars) right back into their purpose and place of ministry! After all, Grace isn't just for fallen church members; it also covers failing and fallen leaders.

This brings us to the critical juncture of praying for our spiritual leaders. Hopefully, the previous statistics coupled with the recent events of fallen ministries, are awakening a burden to intercede for your leaders and believe God to totally restore them in every area they have fallen or are currently struggling.

Chapter 2

COVERING YOUR LEADERS

"You shall make for them linen trousers to cover their nakedness." ~ **Exodus 28:42 NKJV**

The Old Testament reveals that God gave detailed instructions to appointed embroiders to weave linen undergarments to hide the nakedness of the priests who ministered before the Lord. Linen is symbolic of humility, Grace and extravagance. We have been given a royal privilege through prayer to clothe our priests with extravagant Grace. The ministers that labor among us must know they are covered! Even God's most prominent men and women often fall short of people's expectations. That is why God requires the church to pray for them all the more. Those whose mistakes are potentially most visible require a greater amount of prayer covering. God has chosen certain exceptional individuals (our leaders) to be what others *aren't* and to *do* what others *can't*. However, along with the many strengths that leaders posses, they also have many weaknesses. When exceptional people are up they're WAY up and when they're down they're often at rock bottom. The hidden reality is that spiritual fathers grieve when they miss the mark. Their grief is even more deeply felt when their own spiritual sons and daughters malign them. Noah was such a man whose hidden shame was uncovered by his son.

"Noah began farming and planted a vineyard. He drank of the wine and became drunk, and uncovered himself inside his tent. Ham, the father of Canaan, saw the nakedness of his father, and told his two brothers outside. But Shem and Japheth took a garment and laid it upon both their shoulders and walked backward and covered the nakedness of their father; and their faces were turned away, so that they did not see their father's nakedness. When Noah awoke from his wine, he knew what his youngest son had done to him. So he said, "Cursed be Canaan; A servant of servants He shall be to his brothers." He also said, "Blessed be the LORD, the God of Shem; and let Canaan be his servant. May God enlarge Japheth and let him dwell in the tents of Shem; and let Canaan be his servant."
~ Genesis 9:20-27 NASB

Here we see a perfect picture of the way God wants us to respond to a leader's faults. After the flood Noah settled down, like so many leaders after a great victory (see 2 Samuel 11:1-4). After settling down Noah planted a vineyard and became drunk on his own wine. Many leaders today become intoxicated by their own success that they lose their spiritual sensitivity and cannot see the attack of the enemy coming until it's too late and it hits them blindsided. In the shame of His nakedness (I.e. failure, breakdown, burnout), Noah's son Canaan mocks his father by making his shame public to his other two brothers. This is so true of many who focus on a leader's frailties and failures instead of attempting to help cover their leader with prayer and encouragement. Now I want you to see something powerful and for what this book is all about: Shem and Japheth (Noah's other two sons) see their father's nakedness, but instead choose to take a blanket and cover their father's humiliation. O how we need men and women who will take the blanket of prayer and wrap their leaders in fervent intercession.

Upon hearing about Canaan's act of lewdness, Noah curses him. God is not pleased when we make our leader's shame public instead of keeping their weaknesses covered under the God's Grace, loving them regardless, and sincerely and fervently praying for them. On the other hand, Noah blessed Shem and Japheth for their act of honor and respect. God is favorably disposed to the true sons and daughters who cover their spiritual leaders with loyalty and love in spite of their character flaws and leadership blunders.

"Love covers a multitude of sins." ~ **1 Peter 4:8 NASB**

We should also take special consideration that Shem and Japheth walked *backwards* as they carried the blanket to Cover Noah so that they would not be able to look upon his shame. Although our leaders will often reveal very noticeable character flaws, we must not focus upon their weaknesses (places of shame). Rather we must take a strong position to watch the back of our leaders. This way we can be certain to remain sensitive to the possible attacks that will come to them. We must keep watch over our pastors and remain alert to the enemy's scheme (See Ephesians 6:11). The word 'scam' comes from the word 'scheme' and from the beginning satan sets out to make a 'scam' out of our leaders. Remember, as a pastor goes so goes the church. Therefore, we must protect them in prayer and keep them covered from behind. One of the duties appointed to a watchman in Bible times was to stand guard on the wall of the city and sound the alarm (blow the shofar) if an enemy attack was imminent. These men were chosen for their fierce loyalty to the king and the state of affairs of their nation. Likewise, we are accountable to God to faithfully cover and watch the back of our leaders for approaching enemies.

"If the watchman sees the sword coming and does not blow the trumpet and the people are not warned, and a sword comes and takes a person from them... his blood I will require from the watchman's hand." ~ **Ezekiel 33:6 NASB**

Whenever a soldier in the Special Forces or a police officer is engaged in a conflict with someone who is considered "armed and dangerous," he firmly exclaims to his partner, *"Cover me!"* By saying this he trusts his comrade to stay on the lookout and to have his weapon aimed and ready to protect him in the event that he comes under enemy fire. The enemy has launched a full-scale attack against ministry leaders in this last prophetic hour. This is because satan senses the triumphant church marching toward her destiny. Make no mistake; soon the church of Jesus Christ will enter her full destiny and be arrayed with the garments of final victory. We stand upon this brink of the final moment of history.

In my 25 plus years of ministry I have rarely seen a successful church that did not have a strongly led, well administrated base of volunteers dedicated to the ministry of prayer for their leaders. There should be no such thing as a church without the ministry of intercession. This should be one of the founding pillars of any church. The sobering truth is prayerless pews make powerless pulpits. Why? Because if leaders aren't hearing from God how then will they convey His message to the people. Ministries that are advancing in Kingdom power have a firestorm of prayers burning beneath them. The prayers of God's people for a church or a ministry is the coal in the furnace that heats the hearts of souls. Thus, if there is much prayer in a church there will be MUCH power in that church. If some prayer then some power and if no prayer then NO POWER. While it is true that revival IS a sovereign work of Grace, the prayers of God's people strike the flame to the fuse. As the prayer fuse is laid, the flame will follow the powdered line to a igniting of explosive power. Then it will continue to the spreading as of a brushfire, consuming all death, darkness and dryness in its path. Some feel *too dry* for revival. Yet, the best conditions for a wildfire is dry brushwood. Dry wood burns best!

"More and better praying will bring the surest and readiest triumph to God's cause; feeble, formal, listless praying brings decay and death. The church has its sheet-anchor in the closet; its magazine stores are there... When the church of God is aroused to its obligation and duties and right faith to claim what Christ has promised 'all things whatsoever' a revolution will take place." ~ **John Foster**

"The gates of hell will not prevail against a praying church." ~ **Cindy Jacobs**

According to studies conducted by The Barna group, approximately 4000 churches in United States close their doors each year. Churches are losing an estimated 2,765,000 people each year to nominalism and secularism. It is hard to believe but approximately fifty percent of all congregations in are either plateauing or declining. Tragic! While churches around the world experience waves of revival outpouring and exponential growth, the church of America is struggling.

"The low, feeble life of the church, the lack of openness to the power of the Holy Spirit for conversion and holiness, is all owing to the lack of prayer." ~ **Andrew Murray**

No weeping saints, no weeping sinners. ~ **Nancy Shavaz**

The fact that you are reading this book may indicate that you are contemplating your role to pray for and lift the hands of those who watch out for your soul (Hebrews 13:17). I believe our Heavenly Father is delighted that you have taken a sincere interest in praying for your leaders. We must ask the Holy

Spirit to tenderize our hearts with a profound concern for those whom labor among us.

"But we request of you, brethren that you appreciate those who diligently labor among you, and have charge over you in the Lord and give you instruction... Brethren, pray for us."
~ 1 Thessalonians 5:12, 25 NASB

"To this end also we pray for you always, that our God will count you worthy of your calling, and fulfill every desire for goodness and the work of faith with power."
~ 2 Thessalonians 1:11 NASB)

"Pray for us, for we are sure that we have a good conscience, desiring to conduct ourselves honorably in all things." ~
Hebrews 13:18 NASB

Paul wrote in his first letter to the Corinthians that he had a wide-open opportunity for ministry but there were many adversaries lurking and working to prevent him from entering through the "effective" door.

"For a wide door for effective service has opened to me, and there are many adversaries." ~ **1 Corinthians 16:9 NASB**

THE MESSAGE translation of this passage renders the word "adversaries" as "mushrooming opposition." Paul's adversaries mostly consisted of religious, factitious Jews who violently opposed His preaching of the gospel of Grace. Paul (the apostle of Grace) often pleaded with the early church to pray for him on several fronts:

For new, doors to preach the gospel (Colossians 4:3)

For wisdom & clarity in preaching (Ephesians 6:19)

To be fearless in hostile environments (Ephesians 6:19)

For the expansion of his ministry (2 Thessalonians 3:1)

For the receptivity of his audience (2 Thessalonians 3:1)

For deliverance from evil men (2 Thessalonians 3:2)

For his ministry to be accepted (Romans 15:31)

For safe travel and joyful fellowship (Romans 15:32)

For deliverance from severe hardships (2 Corinthians 1:11)

For release from prison (Philemon 1:22)

For loneliness (Romans 15:32; Hebrews 13:9)

To all of these and more we must intercede for God to intervene and empower His servants as they endeavor to extend His kingdom on the earth. Through prayer we will see the strong arm of the Lord extended through our leaders as they fulfill the call of God on their lives.

Someone once said of Charles Wesley, *"He thought prayer to be more his business than anything else."* Your leaders desperately need your investment of time in intercession. There is NO OTHER IMPORTANT ASPECT of the ministry. Heartfelt prayer *bends* the ear of God. That is why I am dedicated to helping raise up end-time prayer partners for God appointed and anointed leaders. I have seen many ministry leaders needlessly struggle in their ministries due to a lack of sufficient prayer covering. Spiritual shepherds need our consistent, fervent, unified and faith-filled prayer.

"God does nothing except in answer to believing prayer."
~ John Wesley

The way to the sheep is through the shepherd. One of satan's strategies is to divide and conquer. If satan can destroy the credibility of our spiritual leaders then he has a better chance to penetrate the lines of our covering and cause more harm to the sheep.

"And Jesus said to them, "You will all fall away, because it is written, 'I WILL STRIKE DOWN THE SHEPHERD, AND THE SHEEP SHALL BE SCATTERED.'" **~ Mark 14:27 NASB**

This interesting United States historical account is such a powerful example of the critical role of praying for our spiritual leaders:

"Early in American history, the British army was at war with America. The setting for this story is the famous Battle of New Orleans. Andrew Jackson, an American General, had been training a group of sharpshooters who had become skilled in hitting their targets at great distances. When the British lined up to attack, Jackson gave the order, "Take out the officers." Soon, British officers were falling from their horses to the ground in great numbers, and the British troops were in disarray. They were 'like sheep without a shepherd.' America won because the British officers were dead or

wounded and no one was in command to give battle instructions... Satan has a battle plan. It is to take out the leaders... Some have fallen into strange and unusual sins. Others have seen strife come in their homes, and their companions tell them they no longer want to be in the ministry... We must remember that everyone, especially spiritual leaders, are subject to the attacks of the enemy. Leaders make decisions that can affect entire nations for the gospel. People support ministries because they trust the persons directing these ministries. We must pray for our leaders to remain strong in spirit, soul and body. We must pray for them to be protected from the strange attacks of the enemy. When satan attempts to 'take out an officer,' we must be present to pray for and help restore these wounded men and women... May it be that satan will say, "That bunch of prayer warriors have knocked another hole in my front line!"

True spiritual leaders may not express it adequately enough but deep inside they highly value the ministry of true intercession. This is because they know if it weren't for those whom sacrificed their own agendas to pray for them, they would not be the men and women they are today. I can totally attest to this fact. I have learned after many years in the ministry that one of the quickest ways for fallen ministers to get back up on their feet is for prayer warriors to get down on their knees. And they will get back up with unshakable resolve when we pray for them with determined authority, not with an *"I hope it will happen"* kind of prayer. We must literally expect that our leader's lives will be a living response of what we declare.

> *"A contending house of prayer doesn't just ask God for answers, but they proclaim a prophetic, authoritative declaration in prayer."* ~ **Lou Engle**

The simple yet profound truth is God uses the prayers you pray for your leaders to help shape history... HIS STORY! What part of His story will you be a part of?

> *"The church holds the balance of power in world affairs... Even now, in this present throbbing moment, by means of her prayer power and the extent to which she uses it, the praying church is actually deciding the course of human events."*
> ~ **Paul Billheimer**

> *"God shapes the world by prayer."* ~ **E.M. Bounds**

Chapter 3

OUR RELATIONSHIP TO OUR LEADERS

"God never gives us discernment in order that we may criticize, but that we may intercede."

~ Oswald Chambers

This chapter focuses on those who are praying or who are considering making a serious commitment to praying for their leaders. Although the subject of praying for our spiritual leaders is of vital concern it also raises many questions and apprehensions such as:

What if my leader is struggling with major sin?

What if my leader is not receptive to wise counsel nor holds himself accountable to leadership?

What if my leader has hurt me or others close to me?

What if my leader is failing to be effective and bring positive, necessary change?

What if my leader isn't interested in my valid and insightful thoughts about his ministry or leadership?

What if I am disappointed in my leader and convinced that he will not respond to the Holy Spirit's guidance?

Concerns like these, our attitudes and the way we relate to our spiritual leaders highly impact the way we pray for them. Before we address the critical nature of effectively praying for our spiritual leaders we must examine our hearts in relationship toward them (1 Thessalonians 5:21).

Finding Faults in Our Leaders

"Discernment is God's call to intercession, never to faultfinding." ~ **Corrie Ten Boom**

I once heard it said that if you're going to lead the orchestra you're going to have to turn your back on the crowd. This statement is so true of leaders. Often leaders feel alone and uncertain. The higher you go as a leader the greater chance you are to be misunderstood, picked apart and maligned. All too often leaders are mocked in a humorous way but for the most part to their shame and hurt. This is mostly due to envy and jealousy. Some say imitation is the greatest form of flattery but often it does not flatter; it stings. Sometimes it seems effortless to find faults in our leaders. In fact, many people tend to incline their opinions towards criticizing rather

46

than affirming (focusing on the negative rather than the positive). One reason for this is because we often recognize the same faults in our own lives and can quickly point it out in others. We must remember that our leaders have the capacity to fail just like us.

"No institution can possibly survive if it needs geniuses or supermen to manage it. It must be organized in such a way as to be able to get along under a leadership composed of average human beings." ~ **Peter Drucker**

Another reason we often find fault is because we secretly harbor envy towards our leaders. Let's face it; many times we point out the mistakes of others to make ourselves feel more secure about who we are and what we've done. Even though God's favor was upon Joseph, his brothers were enraged because of his prophetic dreams of promotion. Look what they did...

"Because the patriarchs were jealous of Joseph, they sold him as a slave into Egypt. But God was with him." ~ **Acts 7:9 NIV**

Jesus was also no stranger to false accusation, misunderstanding and slander. He was the perfect Son of God and yet people still perceived Him to be full of faults. He was vehemently opposed by the religious leaders and even murdered in a jealous rage.

"For He was aware that the chief priests had handed Him over because of envy." ~ **Mark 15:10 NASB**

The Apostle Paul, one of the greatest spiritual leaders of all-time and ordained by God, was viciously attacked by his accusers.

"But when the Jews saw the multitudes, they were filled with envy; and contradicting and blaspheming, they opposed the things spoken by Paul." ~ **Acts 13:45 NKJV**

Criticizing Our Leaders

"Then you will call, and the LORD will answer; you will cry, and He will say, 'Here I am.' If you remove the yoke from your midst, the pointing of the finger and speaking wickedness."
~ Isaiah 58:9 NASB

The dictionary defines the word "criticize" as: to censure, to judge or discuss the merits or faults of to find fault and to judge unfavorably or harshly. God will not answer the prayers of those holding onto a critical spirit. Theirs is the paralysis of analysis. In other words, a faultfinding individual is unable to proceed in his own growth and maturity. Why? Criticism is the sin of speaking wickedness. It places a yoke of bondage upon those who wield it. Your Judgment on your leaders is an open invitation for judgment upon you.

"Do not judge so that you will not be judged. For in the way you judge, you will be judged; and by your standard of measure, it will be measured to you. Why do you look at the speck that is in your brother's eye, but do not notice the log that is in your own eye? Or how can you say to your brother,

Let me take the speck out of your eye, and behold, the log is in your own eye?" ~ **Matt 7:1-4 NASB**

Criticism also has the power to emotionally and spiritually demobilize leaders, leaving them temporarily ineffective for service. Criticism cripples the spirit. As a spiritual leader I have had my share of the pain of people's criticisms. Many times criticism comes in the guise of a *"suggestion for improvement"* or an *"observation."* Yet no matter how you slice it, it's usually criticism. Truth is, you cannot disguise self-righteous criticism and faultfinding.

"If Christians would seriously begin to intercede they would soon find less to criticize." ~ **Derek Prince**

Leadership draws public scrutiny out of people like nothing else. However, one moment in the shoes of a leader and one will find themselves quickly rescinding their selfish opinions. The fact is, wherever there is a leader there is criticism. It's like the old motto says, If you want to be on the stage you have to put up with the drama or if you want to direct the orchestra you have to turn your back on the crowd. When leaders stand before disenchanted, disapproving people it is much more difficult to release ministry than when they are being strongly affirmed. When a leader knows he's losing in the public opinion poll it brings disappointment, discouragement and ultimately causes a leader to throw in the towel. The children of Israel sorely grieved God with their constant murmurings and contemptuous uprisings. Their unthankful and critical nature of

Moses' leadership eventually prevented their generation from inheriting the Promised Land.

"And you GRUMBLED in your tents and said, 'Because the LORD hates us, He has brought us out of the land of Egypt to deliver us into the hand of the Amorites to destroy us. Where can we go up? Our brethren have made our hearts melt, saying, 'the people are bigger and taller than we; the cities are large and fortified to heaven and besides, we saw the sons of the Anakim there... Then the LORD heard the sound of your words, and He was angry and took an oath, saying, 'Not one of these men, this evil generation, shall see the good land which I swore to give your fathers.'" ~ **Deuteronomy 1:27-35 NASB**

"How often they rebelled against Him in the wilderness and grieved Him in the desert! Again and again they tempted God, and pained the Holy One of Israel." ~ **Psalms 78:40-41 NASB**

A critical and complaining attitude (spirit) displeases God and grieves the Holy Spirit. It also delays us from entering into the promotion that God has for us. We also need to be unmistakably aware that the magnitude of our criticism toward our leaders (or anyone for that matter) will determine the measure that will be *multiplied* back to us.

"Do not judge and you will not be judged; and do not condemn, and you will not be condemned; pardon and you will be pardoned. Give and it will be given to you. They will pour into your lap a good measure--pressed down, shaken together,

and running over. For by your standard of measure it will be measured to you in return." ~ **Luke 6:37-38 NASB**

Many times we have interpreted Luke 6:38 to be about giving financially into the church. However, in the context of this passage it directly refers to the way we hand out criticism or forgiveness. When we freely hand out criticism and judgment, it will come back to us in the same measure. This is one of the 3,000 promises in God's word and it is an unfailing promise. Criticizers beware! However we should also be aware that with the measure we forgive the same measure will be returned. Therefore, it pays to continually release forgiveness and be amply generous with our consideration and concession. The Bible is clear on this.

"Blessed are the merciful, for they shall obtain mercy."
~ **Matthew 5:7 NKJV**

Attacking Our Leaders

It is a serious thing to accuse and attack our leaders. In Numbers 16 Korah, one of the family heads of the tribe of Levi, along with Dathan, Abiram and another 250 prominent leaders of the congregation of Israel, conspired against Moses to overthrow him and instate themselves as the new leaders of God's people. Upon hearing this, Moses fell on his face and began to intercede for the people because he knew it would invoke the wrath of God.

"Now Korah... with Dathan and Abiram... and On... took action and they rose up before Moses, together with some of the sons of Israel, two hundred and fifty leaders of the congregation, chosen in the assembly, men of renown. They assembled together against Moses and Aaron, and said to them, "You have gone far enough, for all the congregation are holy, every one of them, and the LORD is in their midst; so why do you exalt yourselves above the assembly of the LORD?" When Moses heard this he fell on his face"
~ Numbers 16:1-4 NASB

This action incurred God's anger and in the remaining verses (Numbers 16:5-35) commands Moses to have the sons of Korah stand before their tents the next morning and hold their censers full of incense. He also instructed the other 250 men to bring their fire-pans near the entrance of tabernacle. The next morning as these men indignantly presented themselves before the tent of meeting; the fury of God came in full force as He mustered a category seven earthquake and the ground completely swallowed the sons of Korah, their homes, their wives, their children and all they owned. How's that for a groundbreaking ceremony? As for the rest of the chiefs of Israel, God's fire thrashed out of their censers and completely engulfed and consumed the entire company (250 people) and all in their path.

We must also take into the account the story of Aaron and Miriam in Numbers 12:1-15 when they openly contested Moses being married to an Ethiopian woman. As a result, God caused Miriam to immediately contract the deadly disease of leprosy. At the end of the account they repented and God healed Miriam and lovingly restored them back to the assembly (Thank God for His everlasting mercy).

We learn a great deal about proper protocol from these stories. Please understand that I am not saying God will consume us with a literal fire or give us a deadly disease when we question, disagree or refute our spiritual leaders. However, we must be careful to respect a holy God, His perfect wisdom and His sovereign decision to appoint certain leaders. After all, God is ultimately the One who appoints our leaders and they ultimately will answer to God for their own actions (and so will we)!

> *"Every person is to be in subjection to the governing authorities. For there is no authority except from God and those which exist are established by God."*
> ~ **Romans 13:1 NASB**

When we conspire against God's leaders and even go as far as to initiate divisive insurrections, we in-effect usurp God's decision to instate a leader and ultimately will answer to Him. Leaders aren't perfect and will often say and do things in which we disagree. However, the proper way to challenge the process with a leader is in a loving and private manner in order to accomplish the following:

> *Allow for explanation regarding all decisions.*
>
> *Avoid public embarrassment where possible.*
>
> *Sincerely express concerns one on one.*

Create a platform for mutual understanding and reconciliation.

How can we pray for our leaders one minute and curse them the next? Every time we curse our leaders, we cancel out the prayers we pray for them. We cannot pray and curse; we can only pray and bless. Cursing neutralizes blessing and vice versa. Furthermore, God does not listen to our prayers when bitterness springs forth from our lips.

"From the same mouth come both blessing and cursing. My brethren, these things ought not to be this way. Does a fountain send out from the same opening both fresh and bitter water?" ~ **James 3:10-11 NASB**

When we secretly or publicly denounce our leaders, we refute God's ability to choose who will lead over us. More than often (as proven throughout Biblical history) God purposely instates leaders who fall very short of man's standards or who do not possess the "necessary qualifications" in order that the glory be not of man but of God.

"God hath chosen the foolish things of the world to confound the wise; and God hath chosen the weak things of the world to confound the things which are mighty."
~ 1 Corinthians 1:27 KJV

God wants us to learn to trust Him and simply pray for our leaders. Prayer moves the heart of God, which in turn moves the arm of man. If you see faults in the lives of your leaders this is to our advantage. Why? It is because it gives God the opportunity to work through our leader's deficiencies.

Remember that we also have grievous faults and that if it weren't for the Grace of God we would be in a horrible mess ourselves. When we pray for our leaders, God can change their heart and when God's changes the heart of a leader He can change the hearts of the people.

When Leaders Hurt Us

Many times in the past I have been deeply hurt by certain leaders. However, thanks to God's Grace and the power of forgiveness I have been healed and made stronger in the process. One thing is certain, bitter people are never better. That's why I made a decision a long time ago that when I am hurt by a leader, I will make every effort to live in the victorious power of God and overcome every attack on my life through trust in God and total forgiveness.

"The greater the hurt, the greater the blessing that will come with forgiveness" ~ **R.T. Kendall**

On the flip side I must sadly admit that I have also hurt others by my own mistakes in leadership. Oh how I wish I could take so many moments back in my life. Although I've done my best to repent where possible I know that I won't be able to redeem every circumstance and person wounded by my lack of wisdom in dealing with people. I look forward to the day when God will allow me to stand before those I've hurt in Heaven and embrace them in the eternal joy of our Lord and Savior.

David was such a man who was hurt by his leader. You see he was on the run from a jealous and evil King Saul who recognized David's anointing and God's favor to be Israel's new leader. Through his hatred and jealousy, King Saul drove David into exile, hunted him down like a dog and had every intention on killing him. Yet David recognized God's call and anointing on Saul's life and continued to respect him even in his confusion and despair. In 1 Samuel 24 David is hiding from King Saul and during the night Saul enters the cave not privy to David's presence. As Saul enters the cave David's men say something like this, *"Hey David, now's your chance! You can take Saul out! No more running, no more eating cactus and grass, no more sleeping on the cold ground. You don't have to take this abuse anymore. Kill him and be done with it."* Is it any wonder why called David a man after His own heart (1 Samuel 13:14). Even though David knew he had legal grounds to dethrone Saul, he yet refused to take matters into his own hands. David did not allow himself to react impulsively against King Saul. The only thing he did was cut off the edge of Saul's robe as proof that he had the opportunity to slay him but in his love and respect for God he chose to be the bigger man.

"Now afterward David arose and went out of the cave and called after Saul, saying, "My lord the king!" And when Saul looked behind him, David bowed with his face to the ground and prostrated himself. David said to Saul, 'Why do you listen to the words of men, saying, 'Behold, David seeks to harm you? Behold, this day your eyes have seen that the LORD had given you today into my hand in the cave, and some said to kill

you, but my eye had pity on you; and I said, 'I will not stretch out my hand against my Lord, for he is the LORD'S anointed."
~ 1 Samuel 24:8-10 NASB

Even though Saul was defiant to God's directives, David was highly aware of the danger of opposing His ordained leadership. By stretching his hand out against Saul he would have stretched his hand out against God Himself. David trusted God to deal with King Saul and in the end God removed him in His own time and in His own way (1 Samuel 31:1-6; Acts 13:22). God is in control and nothing that comes to us slips past His watchful eye. Whatever happens to us happens only as God permits it to pass through His protective hand (Job 1:8-12). And although we may have been hurt we must pray for Grace and healing from God and continue to do the right thing by praying for our leaders without selfish motive. As we patiently wait for God to deal with the circumstances surrounding the problems with our leadership, we can trust that we will see His faithful hand at work. And to be certain, God does all things well (Mark 7:37).

One of the reasons many people are caught off guard when a leader hurts them is because they perceive leaders as impervious to mistakes from their lofty towers of authority and "Godliness." However, the reality is that leaders are more susceptible to making mistakes and even being hurt because of their greater exposure to people and their idiosyncrasies. Far too often we are completely unaware of the agony our leaders face daily from financial pressures, constant personal assault on their character, deep misunderstanding of their intentions, abandonment and betrayal from friends, slander from people within their own leadership ranks, and many times even crisis in their home. Our leaders sometimes are perceived as being ones who inflict pain but the reality is they are often the ones who bear the most pain. This is because they are the ones who daily confront and carry the deep hurts and unhealed wounds of others!

"All of the great leaders have had one characteristic in common: it was the willingness to confront unequivocally the major anxiety of their people in their time. This, and not much else, is the essence of leadership." ~ **John Kenneth Galbraith**

You may have heard it said that the church would be a great place if it weren't for the people. This may sound cynical but we must remember that wherever there are people there will be problems to be dealt with and *fires* to be put out. Pastors and leaders are many times expected to work out every problem and solve every issue. Be honest; if you were in the leader's shoes, would you be any different than your leader? When God chose great leaders in the Bible, he chose ordinary men, many times with greater flaws than the normal individual. What made these men great was their ability to admit that they were incapable of accomplishing God's purposes in themselves. God doesn't call the qualified. He qualifies the 'called.' God is shaping your leader to be the man or woman that will be worthy to stand before you and you must learn to be patient with Him through the process. The fact that our leaders are human is even greater reason for us to pray for them. For it is only through the power of God that they will be empowered to minister and lead. Remember, just because our leaders are chosen by God doesn't mean they do everything perfectly. But rest assured, God is maturing our leaders for the task of leading those who are themselves maturing.

Chapter 4

OUR RESPONSIBILITY TO OUR LEADERS

"Let the elders who rule well be counted worthy of double honor, especially those who labor in the word and doctrine." ~ **1 Timothy 5:17 NKJV**

The way in which we respond to our leaders is of critical importance in the mind-set of those who pray for them. Regardless of our feelings toward our leaders we are nevertheless still responsible to pray for them. By doing this, we can have an impact through our leaders to exercise a decisive influence upon our culture. Our prayer for our leaders should be: *"Lord, empower our leaders to the extent that for Your glory alone, we can experience victory through their ministry."* Remember that by praying for your leaders, you are a direct recipient of what flows out of them. That is why our responses and actions toward our leaders are so critical. Although it is normal to have certain feelings about our leaders (negative or positive), it is our reactions towards our leaders that either cause bitterness, contempt, or attract the Grace of God in our lives. If we remain embittered toward our leaders and cease to pray for them, we allow for 'breaches' in the wall of defense. It would be likened to a watchman abandoning his post and allow for enemy invasion. When we have been out-of-sorts with our leaders, our ability to pray for them is weakened. However, if we look past our own feelings and remain loyal to God's purposes, our prayers can literally help to attract the Grace of God upon the life of our leaders and ultimately to those whom they minster to.

"Let no corrupt word proceed out of your mouth, but what is good for necessary edification, that it may impart Grace to the hearers." ~ **Ephesians 4:29 NKJV**

Honoring Our Leaders

Firstly, we are called by God not only to honor our leaders but to give them *double honor!* This is especially true regarding those who spiritually lead us. With leadership comes the increased challenges of public scrutiny and defamation of character. Unfortunately, when a person becomes a threat in the Kingdom of God they automatically become the target of the enemy (and even often) the very people they lead. Whenever someone is given a position of public authority, it becomes more difficult to hide who they really are. The truth is the higher leaders go, the more frightening it can become. That is why it is so easy to see the faults of our spiritual leaders. Have you ever stopped to consider that your leaders are human just like you are? Where is the Grace that we should be showing our leaders? The truth is we actually empower our leaders by allowing them the margin to fail. And believe me, they will fail. However, when our leaders don't live up to our expectations and make the *common* mistakes (that we make ourselves) we should lovingly and prayerfully help to encourage and restore them.

"Brethren, if a man is overtaken in any trespass, you who are spiritual restore such a one in a spirit of gentleness, considering yourself lest you also be tempted."
~ Galatians 6:1 NKJV

On a side note: I am not saying that we should tolerate or accept a lifestyle of sin from our leaders It is important for leaders to live their lives in such a way that if their lives today were made headline news tomorrow there would be no reason for shame. Leaders will never be able to rise above the level of their own character. Often the reason why God does not allow leaders promotion and access into greater spheres of influence is because their character does not exceed the level of their leadership. Talent alone is not enough for leadership. Talent may take you to the top but character will sustain you there. In all these regards, we must nevertheless pray fervently for our leaders. Being able to love in spite of being hurt, offended or confused by our leaders shows maturity in our

Affirming Our Leaders

An affirming atmosphere breeds an empowered leader. Ministers covered in affirmation perform at optimal level where an ambiance of encouragement is being fostered. The New Testament speaks of a mighty evangelist by the name of Apollos (See Acts 18:24-28). Upon his arrival to preach at the church at Ephesus, he began to exhort the people. Some present had found out he had not yet been baptized in the Holy Spirit. The passage goes on to say that Priscilla and Aquila pulled him aside and began to explain the scriptures "more accurately" to him (regarding the infilling of the Holy Spirit). For a moment consider how this may have made Apollos feel. What would some of us feel like when someone tries to explain things "more accurately" to us? Would we feel inadequate, less knowledgeable, stupid, vulnerable, unsure of ourselves, or all of the above? I'm sure you could fill in the blanks with some other choice words. However, could it be that some present at Ephesus might have picked up on this? Before Apollos departed for his next assignment some members of the congregation began to encourage him and look what happens next:

"And when he (Appolos) wanted to go across to Achaia, THE BRETHREN ENCOURAGED HIM and wrote to the disciples to welcome him; and when he arrived he greatly helped those who had believed... for he powerfully refuted the Jews in public, demonstrated by the Scriptures that Jesus was the Christ." ~ Acts 18:27-28 NASB

It is apparent that Apollos so vivaciously demonstrated the power of God in his ministry following his visit at Ephesus was because he most likely had received the word given by Priscilla and Aquila and was baptized in the Holy Spirit (we can assume this by the context of scripture). However, we cannot dispute in verse 27 that as the people sent Apollos on his way with a good dose of encouragement it also contributed greatly to His success (verse 28).

Submitting to Our leaders

We have been called by God to submit to our leaders. This doesn't mean we are to do everything they say and give absolute, unobjectionable, blind obedience to their commands. Absolving to this kind of submission leads to error both on the part of the follower and of the leader. However, Godly submission includes possessing a gentle spirit with a willingness to prefer a leader's direction, even if it goes against our opinion. After all submission isn't submission until we disagree on the matter. In the meantime we must wait on God's guidance, trusting that He will bring a leader under His correction in His timing.

"Obey your leaders and SUBMIT to them, for they keep watch over your souls as those who will give an account. Let them do this with joy and not with grief, FOR THIS WOULD BE UNPROFITABLE FOR YOU." ~ **Hebrews 13:17 NASB**

The way in which we respond to our leaders will either be *beneficial* or otherwise *unprofitable* for us. If we curse, condemn, criticize, accuse or mistreat them with our words and actions, we will eventually be reciprocates of the negative effects of their leadership. Leaders go where they are celebrated and tend to lead by the way they are empowered to lead. Truth is, leaders lead only as well as their followers allow them to lead. Any great leader leads greatly only because the people give them the sincere loyalty and courtesy to lead them. Thus, leaders will have a *hard row to hoe* unless the people agree with God and graciously allow them to lead. If we submit to our spiritual leaders, even as we clearly recognize their humanity. God's Grace will have a much better chance of manifesting in their lives, empowering them to shepherd us in God's love and authority. Truth is, submission isn't submission until you disagree. As we submit and patiently wait on God, He will give us Grace and change our own hearts in the process as He lovingly deals with the hearts of our leaders

Understanding Our Leaders

Our spiritual leaders greatly need our understanding and patience. However, we are naturally prone to impatience and the immediate demand that leaders *measure up* to our expectations, meet all our needs and answer all our questions. Yet, far too often spiritual leaders are faced with tremendous uncertainty and need divine insight to the overwhelming challenges they face (that challenge may even be you). Imagine the pressure Moses must have felt as he approached a dead end at the Red Sea. His dire circumstance required a miracle and yet all the grumbling Israelites could think of was themselves.

"Hence God led the people around by the way of the wilderness to the Red Sea; and the sons of Israel went up in martial array from the land of Egypt... Then they said to Moses, "Is it because there were no graves in Egypt that you have taken us away to die in the wilderness? Why have you dealt with us in this way, bringing us out of Egypt? Is this not the word that we spoke to you in Egypt, saying, 'Leave us alone that we may serve the Egyptians'? For it would have been better for us to serve the Egyptians than to die in the wilderness." But Moses said to the people, "Do not fear! Stand by and see the salvation of the LORD, which He will accomplish for you today; for the Egyptians whom you have seen today, you will never see them again forever. The LORD will fight for you WHILE YOU KEEP SILENT."
~ Exodus 13:18; 14:11-14 NASB

Our leaders need compassion and understanding for their situation just as we do. As we privately and mercifully intercede for our leaders, God will arise in the situation and give solutions to otherwise unsolvable problems.

Forgiving Our Leaders

We must accept the fact that sooner or later leaders may eventually disappoint and even hurt us. That is because they are human (just like us). However, if we were all honest with ourselves, we can probably recount a time when we have all offended or hurt someone. To weave through the shifting dynamics of our relationships to our leaders, we must prepare our heart to walk in forgiveness BEFORE our leaders have the chance to offend us. Jesus warned us that it was impossible NOT be offended.

"Then He said to the disciples, 'It is impossible that no offenses should come.' " ~ **Luke 17:1 NKJV**

This passage clearly tells us that it is absolutely impossible for offenses not to come to us. However, there is a strong principle in God's word that helps us to confront and deal with the pain we have experienced by our leaders. It is found in Jesus own words.

"Whenever you stand praying, forgive, if you have anything against anyone, so that your Father who is in heaven will also forgive you your transgressions. But if you do not forgive, neither will your Father who is in heaven forgive your transgressions." ~ **Mark 11:25-26 NASB**

Forgiveness affects the outcome or non-outcome of our prayers. If we pray for our leaders with unforgiveness in our heart, our prayers will have no affect for them. We must also understand that our own breakthrough is bound or released by forgiveness. The verses just prior to Mark 11:25 tell us that if we speak to our mountains, they will be removed and cast into the sea (Read Mark 11:23-24). However, our mountain being removed is contingent upon whether or not we obey Mark 11:25: *"Whenever you stand praying, forgive if you have anything against anyone."* Our freedom and deliverance is directly linked to our ability to forgive those whom have hurt us. We must also consider that many times we really have no grounds to be offended. Too often our leaders haven't hurt us, we simply imagine that they have. This is critical to understand here. We often tie our own issues of abandonment and entitlement to our leaders. If we have been hurt in the past by other *father figures* in our lives, then our expectations of our spiritual leaders can often be unrealistic. When they fail us, it triggers that wounded place in us. If a leader ignores us, then *obviously* they must have ought against us. This is most often entirely untrue and simply a distorted perception. To those feeling hurt or abandoned, perception is reality. Again, it's mostly an issue of our imagination. That is why the apostle Paul tells us to cast down faulty imaginations and submit them to Jesus (2 Corinthians 10:5). The problem often isn't with our leaders; it's with US. That is why we must settle the identity crisis issue once and for all. Our identity is not in whether or not our leaders value or accept us. We must find total acceptance from our Heavenly Father and believe what He thinks and feels about us (Jeremiah 29:11). Our Father loves us and has a spectacular future in store for us. We must lean solely on His affirmation and approval. We are completely covered by His Grace. When we learn to place all our insecurities in Him, we won't be driven by the need to rely on attention, value or significance from our leaders. In this way, we can powerfully pray for our leaders without the sting of offense that ultimately hinders our prayers and continues to drive a wedge in our relationships with them. Therefore, the best way to keep our leaders from grieving us to the point of despair is to choose to forgive them before they have the chance to hurt us (albeit if they do). Unforgiveness may hurt our leaders initially but it will do much more damage to us in the long run. Unforgiveness is the incubator for painful disappointment. However, if we forgive our leaders BEFORE they hurt us, then we will not be disappointed when they do. I also believe that as we pray for our leaders, we are supernaturally empowered to forgive them. In fact, praying for our leaders is the proof of our forgiveness. The power of forgiveness profoundly enables us to pray more powerfully for our leaders regardless of what they may say or do to us. What a joy to get caught up in this cycle. Forgiveness disarms our enemy and relinquishes his emotional, psychological and spiritual control over our life. It empowers us to love like we've never been hurt. We must guard our heart against resentment toward our leaders and instead pray for them in love, faith and power! (Proverbs 4:23,24) We'll be the better for it and so will our leaders!

"The Person who gains the most forgiveness is the person who does the forgiving." ~ **R.T. Kendall**

"When you forgive, you in no way change the past but you sure do change the future. " ~ **Bernard Meltzer**

"Father, forgive them; for they know not what they do."
~ **Luke 23:34 KJV**

Chapter 5

HOW TO PRAY FOR OUR LEADERS

"Now I urge you, brethren, by our Lord Jesus Christ and by the love of the Spirit, to strive together with me in your prayers to God for me, that I may be rescued from those who are disobedient in Judea, and that my service for Jerusalem may prove acceptable to the saints; so that I may come to you in joy by the will of God and find refreshing rest in your company."

~ Romans 15:30-32

To more fervently understand and accurately pray for our leaders, we must follow Biblical models of praying for our leaders. The Apostle Paul wrote to the church at Rome and outlined seven prayer requests that are significantly relative to today's leaders. Our hearts will be more stirred toward our leaders when we pray for them no

71

matter what opinions we may hold of them. It is difficult to maintain a distant or contemptuous attitude toward our leaders when we pray for them.

1. Pray Deeply and Sincerely for Your Leader

Paul asks the church in Rome "...*strive together with me in your prayers to God for me...*" By the context of this passage, Paul seems to have been in an intense spiritual struggle. The Greek word for *'strive together'* is *'sunagonidzomai'* derived from two Greek words *('sun' & 'agonidzo')*. The Greek word *'sun'* means *'with'* or *'together.'* Unity releases an anointing for breakthrough and many times when people come together to pray they inspire each other with thoughts and revelations that bring the release our leaders need. Therefore leaders need to schedule special times (preferably regularly) for their team to come together and spend quality time praying for the needs of the leader.

The word *'agonidzo'* carries the same weight as if our heart deeply ached for the other person as we contend for them in prayer. Paul instructed the church in Rome to literally and physically pray deeply with sincerity. This is a level of intercession that cannot be attained instantly but takes time in the presence of the Holy Spirit. It is rare to find people who know of this type of praying. Saints of old are very familiar on this turf and it would behoove many of us to become more acquainted with those who pray in this fashion. We can all learn from these seasoned saints: the kind of folks that know how to pray "ugly." There is something fascinating about an older prayer warrior when he or she opens their mouth and the entire room comes to attention. We as leaders need to have someone in our lives that can pray over us in this way; a saint who can pack a punch in the spirit. We don't need pretty poetic prayers prayed over us when we're in a crisis. We need people who are not afraid to lay hands on us, mightily intercede and pull the Heavens down on our behalf.

> *"The effective, fervent prayer of a righteous man avails much."* ~ **James 5:16 NKJV**

Some translations of the words "effectual fervent" are "boiling hot." When we pray confident in our right standing with God our prayers become boiling hot. Our confidence should never be in our prayers or in how we pray them but rather in the God who answers them. God doesn't come through for us because we are faithful but because HE is faithful. That's why the scripture instructs us to cast all our worries, burdens, anxieties, concerns, problems, troubles, issues and circumstances on God when we pray (1 Peter 5:7). Faith in God's promises get's God's attention and moves Him to action on our behalf. This is not to say that more exertion gets more results when we pray but when you're in a crisis and you are desperate for an answer you will pray with fervent intensity as if your life depended on it. The attitude of fervent prayer is to call on God as if EVERYTHING depended on God (and it certainly does). Again, sincerity is the key word. I also believe it is important not to pray out of anxiety but out of faith. Many people *fray* instead of pray. Anxious prayers accomplish nothing. We must be at peace with our righteousness position with God based on His finished work in our life and rely on His desire to *do for us* rather than our desire to *do for Him*. When we pray in this way, our faith is ignited and we will certainly see results.

2. Pray with a 'Vengeance' for Your Leaders

Upon receiving the news of Peter being thrown into prison facing impending execution for preaching the gospel, the church gathered for prayer (Acts 12:1-19). This prayer meeting was scheduled at Mary's house (who was the mother of John Mark) to pray that Peter would be released from prison. The scriptures indicate that it wasn't just a casual gathering.

"So Peter was kept in the prison, but prayer for him was being MADE FERVENTLY BY THE CHURCH to God... to the house of Mary, the mother of John who was also called Mark, where many were gathered together and were praying."
~ Acts 12:5, 12 NASB

Many had convened to pray at Mary's house and the atmosphere was intense. We must be aware that our leaders often face crisis that threatens to tear their families and ministries apart. This requires more than a social club gathering to chat about the current issues. A serious and dedicated prayer team should be at the helm to call an emergency prayer session on behalf of our leaders. And their presence should frighten hell.

Meanwhile back at the prison, look what happens as the people are praying…

"So Peter was kept in the prison, but prayer for him was being made fervently by the church to God. On the very night when Herod was about to bring him forward, Peter was sleeping between two soldiers, bound with two chains, and guards in front of the door were watching over the prison. And behold, an angel of the Lord suddenly appeared and a light shone in the cell; and he struck Peter's side and woke him up, saying, "Get up quickly." And his chains fell off his hands."
~ Acts 12:5-7 NASB

Many had convened to pray at Mary's house and the atmosphere was intense. We must be aware that our leaders often face crisis that threatens to tear their families and ministries apart. This requires more than a social club gathering to chat about the current issues. A serious and dedicated prayer team should be at the helm to call an emergency prayer session on behalf of our leaders. And their presence should frighten hell.

Meanwhile back at the prison, look what happens as the people are praying…

"So Peter was kept in the prison, but prayer for him was being made fervently by the church to God. On the very night when Herod was about to bring him forward, Peter was sleeping between two soldiers, bound with two chains, and guards in front of the door were watching over the prison. And behold,

an angel of the Lord suddenly appeared and a light shone in
the cell; and he struck Peter's side and woke him up, saying,
"Get up quickly." And his chains fell off his hands."
~ Acts 12:5-7 NASB

The prayers of God's people blast open locked doors for our leaders (Psalms 107:16). Picture it; Peter was chained to two heavily armed Roman centurions and the door was bolted shut. Often just because certain doors are presently locked doesn't mean our leaders aren't supposed to go through those doors. It may be an issue of timing or often the enemy is barring the door for fear that our leaders will possess what waits for them on the other side. That's the way it feels many times for ministers who are trusting God for open doors. We must possess the gates of the enemy through our prayers for our leaders.

Notice also that Peter was on the floor asleep. This may have been because he was discouraged, exhausted, or just flat out defeated. Who knows? Whatever the case, an angel kicked him in the side and commanded him to rise up. Our prayers can awaken dead dreams in our leaders and cause them to reclaim their passion and purpose. Verse 19 says that Herod couldn't even find him once he had escaped. When we come together to pray for our leaders, God will make a way of escape for our leaders and hide them from the schemes of the enemy. The story in Acts 12 ends with Peter being miraculously led by an angel in the middle of the night past two guards, through the iron gates of the prison, right to Mary's house. This is the miraculous power of fervent intercession for our leaders.

In these regards we must consider that our leaders are constantly imposing on the gates of the enemy (Matthew 11:12). Therefore, we must set ourselves in agreement with God's purposes that our leaders will mount a victorious offensive campaign and break through the demonic strongholds that hold souls captive.

"Indeed I will greatly bless you, and I will greatly multiply your seed as the stars of the heavens and as the sand which is on the seashore; AND YOUR SEED SHALL POSSES THE GATE OF THEIR ENEMIES." ~ **Genesis 22:17 NASB**

3. Pray for Your Leader's Relationships

The words *"rescued from those who are disobedient"* from our chapter's key passage (Romans 15:32), indicate that Paul had his share of opposition. We should pray that the right people will enter our leaders' lives and the wrong people will exit their lives. Leaders encounter significant resistance from people attempting to make their ministry difficult (I.e. back-biters, needy people who drain them, false accusers, etc.) Whenever the Lord wants to promote you, He'll send a person into your life. Conversely, when the devil wants to destroy you, he'll send a person into your life as well. We need to make sure that our leaders are spiritually and emotionally protected from those who would fight against the will of God and be a hindrance to their peace of mind and ultimately the advancement of the gospel. When we pray in this way we help to secure a circle of peace around our leaders and release them to lead with clarity of mind and spirit!

Whenever there is increased momentum in a leader's ministry, you can be sure the wrong people will try to enter his life. A leader's intercessor should put a prayer shield up against these types of individuals. They should also be a strong moral support to their leader upholding them in public and private. People will try taking advantage of an opportunity when there is dissention in the ranks. When a leader is strong and confident, the "dissenters" are ineffective. Prayer is the way we empower our leaders to possess unshakable influence.

4. Pray for Your Leader's Effectiveness

Paul pleaded, "...*that my service for Jerusalem may prove acceptable to the saints.*" (Romans 15:31) Many times a leader's prayer team can sense when the pastor or leader is struggling during a sermon and whether or not his message is being received by the people with open hearts. Sometimes a leader is led by God to preach a "controversial" word in order to bring firm resolve to issues that impede forward progress of the Gospel. A word of caution: Strict confidentiality among the pastor's trusted prayer council is critical regarding issues involving rebellion, factions, open sin and division. Although these should be fully addressed, due to the sensitive nature of some allegations, mature discretion must be applied.

5. Pray for Your Leader's Emotions

Paul went on to request, *"that I may come to you in joy"* (Romans 15:32). What minister doesn't want to enjoy his vocation? Ministry can often be more of a burden than a joy. Oh the exhilaration that comes from the fulfillment and satisfaction of a mission accomplished. We should pray that our ministers would experience this kind of joy. Pastors and leaders shouldn't have to accept depression as a way of life. Sure there will be highs and lows, But God wants leaders to experience His life and have it more abundantly in every season of their lives and ministry (John 10:10). Look what Paul had to endure in his ministry:

"Five times I received from the Jews thirty-nine lashes. Three times I was beaten with rods, once I was stoned, three times I was shipwrecked, a night and a day I have spent in the deep. I have been on frequent journeys, in dangers from rivers, dangers from robbers, dangers from my countrymen, dangers from the Gentiles, dangers in the city, dangers in the wilderness, dangers on the sea, dangers among false brethren; I have been in labor and hardship, through many sleepless nights, in hunger and thirst, often without food, in cold and exposure. Apart from such external things, there is the daily pressure on me of concern for all the churches."
~ 2 Corinthians 11:24-25

Is it any wonder why Paul asked the church to pray that he could have some joy? He received the same thirty-nine lashes that Jesus received FIVE separate times! Paul was also stoned, shipwrecked, faced peril from the treacherous terrain he had to travel through, attacked and robbed by bandits and thieves, faced incredible hardship, insomnia, starvation and exposure to fierce weather. On top of all the hell that Paul had to endure, his main concern was the precarious state of the several churches he was overseeing. So you can't blame him for wanting joy. We need to pray for our leaders when they are faced with circumstances that could potentially steal their joy and ask God to fill them with the fullness of His joy as they encounter immense difficulties as soldiers of the light of Jesus.

"Let Your priests be clothed with righteousness, and let Your godly ones sing for joy." ~ **Psalms 132:9 NASB**

6. Pray for Your Leader's Discernment

Paul's desire was to be in the center of God's will. He asked, *"that I may come to you with joy... BY THE WILL OF GOD."* (Romans 15:32b) Many leaders make costly mistakes that derail them from the destiny God intended for them. This is why we must pray that our leaders will make right decisions. The Greek word for *will* is *thelema* meaning *design, purpose or plan.* We must ask God to give our leaders clear *vision* in order to make clear *decisions.* We must pray for them to clearly discern the plan of God. Pray that they remain sensitive to the voice of the Lord and follow His promptings to avoid potential dangers along the way. Many times leaders are uncertain and need a 'word' from God as they publicly minister and privately serve. A wrong decision doesn't affect God but it does affect the people. Our leader's decisions ultimately affect us and that gives us even greater reason to pray for our leaders to make wise choices in all they put their hands to.

7. Pray for Your Leader's Rest

Paul ended his requests for prayer with, *"...and find refreshing rest in your company."* (Romans 15:32c) We all need opportunities to recover from the mental, physical and spiritual exhaustion that life brings. Stress and pressure from the ministry is almost at times unbearable. I once saw a painting of a minister sitting at his desk, completely exhausted with his head down in despair. The painting was remarkably vivid in portraying a pastor who was about to give up. At the bottom half of the picture it showed an angel washing his feet. It was one of the most touching paintings I have ever seen. I often can relate to the minster in the portrait.

When Paul visited the church at Rome again, he didn't want to face a congregation that was frazzled and overwhelmed with issues. He simply wanted to experience God's life with them and enjoy his time with them. He wanted to look forward to his visit and asked them to pray that He would be refreshed upon returning to see them. Ministers want to feel a sense of peace when they are in the company of their people. Often this is not the case. We must learn to take advantage of the Grace of God in our own issues especially when ministers attempt to counsel us through our conflicts. Many times people don't really want to do what their pastors tell them to do, they just want to be heard and dump their struggles on them, thus leaving critical issues unresolved. We need to apply the principles of wisdom our pastors share with us in order to live victoriously. When we neglect or refuse to put into practice the life lessons our leaders give, it creates continued stress and even havoc in our lives and also in the lives of our leaders. Many times, the problem isn't with the Pastor; it's with the congregants who refuse to apply truth.

Also, along with all the continued stresses ministers face, they often neglect vacations and seasons of needed rest because of their tremendous burden for God's people and the ministry. Yet, of all the people who need to learn to rest and enjoy life it's ministers. One of the Godliest things a minister can do is rest.

"I said, "Oh, that I had wings like a dove! I would fly away and be at rest."" ~ **Psalms 55:6 NASB**

The nature of ministry is so extremely demanding and overwhelming at times that ministers have the propensity to absorb the depression, fear, anxiety, sickness, marital strife and all the other difficulties that come from being with sheep. True shepherds smell like their sheep. That's because they are right in the middle of the pasture with the flock; walking through all their stuff with them. After all, true shepherds not only have to lead sheep, they also have to clean their stalls.

We must intercede for our ministers and ask God to provide ample opportunities for restoration, relaxation and recovery. Ministers need a thorough washing and refreshing from the difficulties of ministry on a regular basis. I've even heard of some congregations graciously blessing their pastor with a cruise or a weekend getaway with their spouses. My worship team and choir once did this for my wife and I and I can tell you this left a lasting impression on me and helped me recharge my batteries for the work ahead. It blesses the heart of God when His people not only pray for them to rest but help them find a place of solace. Often we are the answer to our leaders need.

PRAYER FOR YOUR LEADER: *Heavenly Father, please touch my leader in a powerful way right now, this moment! I ask you to let the right people enter his life and the wrong people exit his life. Help him to find the appropriate acceptance from those to whom he ministers and let the words he speaks find a place in their heart so they may apply it to their life and future. Lord, enable the people to apply the wisdom and truth he gives so they may not make his life even more difficult. Help my leader to remain resolute with the word you have given him and help him to humble himself when he has misinterpreted your direction. I ask You to cause him to enjoy what You have called him to. Give him clear vision to make clear decisions and that he will be in the center of Your perfect will for his life, for his family and for his ministry. Give him a special bonus this very day and allow someone somewhere to bless him and his family for all he does for You and for Your people. He well deserves a time of fun and relaxation. Overwhelm him with Your abundant* *goodness today and let him Know that he is deeply loved by You and by those who lift him up in prayer. In the mighty name of Jesus... Amen!*

Chapter 6

WHAT TO PRAY
FOR OUR LEADERS

"We give thanks to God always for all of you, making
mention of you in our prayers."
~ 1 Timothy 1:2 NASB

There is much to pray for in the life of your leader and having a detailed prayer strategy will make your praying much more purposeful and thorough. An important rule of thumb to remember is "Out of sight – Out of mind." This means if you don't have the proper information within sight, you usually won't remember it. That's why it is important to have a written plan of action for praying for your leaders. Although prayer should be a natural and frequent part of every Christian's daily routine, it can easily get neglected. To have an effective prayer ministry for your leaders, it must be led well. We cannot rely on just inspiration to pray which results in prayer only when it feels right or on the heels of crisis. It must also be guided by good old fashioned discipline and well thought out administration. Prayer ministries must not only be inspired by a purpose but also ON PURPOSE. And the truth is if you fail to plan, then you plan to fail.

It is possible to pray effectively in an impromptu and unstructured setting when the situation calls for it. However, most of the time when you don't have a formulated system of prayer in place it often results in non-execution. Good intentions don't always pan out when it comes to prayer. Application and execution are just as important as intention. Therefore, simply adding a plan or a structure to your prayer ministry can greatly benefit, so too can the development of the prayer life of a church through a prayer strategy. For instance, preparing a short document with points or topics will help keep you focused, time conscious and targeted you as you pray.

In order to develop a well-rounded prayer strategy for your leaders, I suggest implementing each one of the following five approaches to prayer as you develop your specific strategy:

Impromptu Prayers

Compounded Prayers

Prayer Specialist

Prayer Schedule

Topical Prayers

Impromptu Prayers

Impromptu praying is praying on the spot. You can be anywhere at anytime and pray for your leaders. To adequately pray for you leaders you must allow God to put His own words into your mouth for the sake of praying in His power. By God's words we are enabled in Holy Spirit power to rule over nations and kingdoms, to break down, destroy and overthrow spiritual strongholds and to build-up and establish God's rule in the lives of our leaders.

> *"Then the LORD stretched out His hand and touched my mouth, and the LORD said to me, "Behold, I have put My words in your mouth. "See, I have appointed you this day over the nations and over the kingdoms, To pluck up and to break down, To destroy and to overthrow, To build and to plant." ~*
> **Jeremiah 1:9-10 NASB**

It is also critical to ask the Holy Spirit to give you prophetic discernment, insight, wisdom and understanding so you can pray in the right timing. Many times we are not clear as how or what we should pray. In fact upon the authority of scripture we don't know how to pray at all (Romans 8:26). You may not always know what your leader is going through but if you seek the Lord diligently and place yourself in a position to receive His guidance, the Holy Spirit will reveal hidden things to you regarding your leader and give immediate understanding on how to pray for your leader and their particular situation.

"But just as it is written, 'THINGS WHICH EYE HAS NOT SEEN AND EAR HAS NOT HEARD, AND which HAVE NOT ENTERED THE HEART OF MAN, ALL THAT GOD HAS PREPARED FOR THOSE WHO LOVE HIM.' For to us God revealed them through the Spirit; for the Spirit searches all things, even the depths of God. For who among men knows the thoughts of a man except the spirit of the man which is in him? Even so the thoughts of God no one knows except the Spirit of God. Now we have received, not the spirit of the world, but the Spirit who is from God, so that we may know the things freely given to us by God, which things we also speak, not in words taught by human wisdom, but in those taught by the Spirit, combining spiritual thoughts with spiritual words."

~ 1 Corinthians 2:9-13 NASB

Often the Holy Spirit will alarm you at any given time at to an urgency to pray for your leader. This has happened to many of my intercessors. Many times I've received calls and texts from my prayer partner regarding critical and sometimes even dire situations at the exact time I was in a pressing situation. God is faithful to alarm His intercessors with needful information relative to a leader's needs.

Compounded Prayers

One main misconception in the subject of praying for your leaders is that God expects you to pray several hours everyday in order to see great results. This is a false expectation unless the Lord specifically speaks to you in this regard. Most often, it is the faithful, consistent and compounded prayers of God's people, over time, that eventually add up to glorious outcomes for your leaders. Having a prayer life is like tending a garden. Sometimes it's tedious and repetitious but you will reap the fruit of your prayers if you have consistently watered the garden of your prayer life. When it's the season for bearing fruit, you will reap the harvest of your prayers if you have maintained a daily walk with God in prayer. Praying consistently is also like depositing money into the bank. When you make consistent deposits of prayer into your savings account in Heaven, you can be sure that you can regularly make handsome withdrawals.

"Let us not lose heart in doing good, for in due time we will reap if we do not grow weary." ~ **Galatians 6:9 NASB**

The important thing to remember when you pray is that God sees you when you pray and He will honor your faithfulness. Although Grace is God's unmerited, unearned and undeserved favor, God DOES reward diligence and obedience. However, it's not the amount of time spent with God daily that gets results. It's the faithful, daily prayers over time that honor God, reap dividends, and bring us to the breakthrough we have believed for.

"He is a rewarder of them that diligently seek Him."
~ Hebrews 11:6 NASB

Another powerful thought regarding compounded prayers is found in the book of Revelation: the concept of filling God's golden vials with the incense our prayers.

*"And when he had taken the book, the four beasts and four and twenty elders fell down before the Lamb, having every one of them harps, and golden vials full of odors, which are the prayers of saints. ~ **Revelation 5:8 KJV**

"Another angel came and stood at the altar, holding a golden censer; and much incense was given to him, so that he might add it to the prayers of all the saints on the golden altar which was before the throne. And the smoke of the incense, with the prayers of the saints, went up before God out of the angel's hand. Then the angel took the censer and filled it with the fire of the altar, and threw it to the earth; and there followed peals of thunder and sounds and flashes of lightning and an earthquake." ~ **Revelation 8:3-5 NASB**

Every time you pray your intercession rises like multi colored vapors of fragrant incense that fill God's vials with the beautiful fragrance of your prayers. When the bowls are about to brim over with prayers, God pours them back onto the earth, only this time they have multiplied in power as they are dumped back upon the earth (specifically for that which you've prayed for) in peals of thunder, flashes of lightning, and earthquakes. Just keep praying for your leaders and wait and see what mighty things God will do. Look what happens when we pray consistently for our leaders:

"Call to Me and I will answer you, and I will tell you great and mighty things, which you do not know... And the Levitical priests shall never lack a man before Me to offer burnt

offerings, to burn grain offerings and to prepare sacrifices
continually." ~ **Jeremiah 33:3,18 NASB**

The key in the above passage is not the length of time that you give to praying for your leaders but rather obedience to the call and the fervent attention in which you give it. When we call on the Lord on behalf of our leaders God ensures us (Verse 18) that we will never have a lack leaders and ministers of integrity who are full of the anointing and favor of God. When we pray for our leaders we help to empower their integrity and longevity.

Prayer Specialist

A *prayer specialist* is someone who chooses to focus his or her prayers on a specific area of a leader's ministry rather than others. For instance, one of my most faithful intercessors has chosen over the years to focus his attention on my family. As a leader I couldn't feel more secure in knowing that my family is constantly blanketed in powerful intercession. As a recipient of this type of praying I can say with experience that this is a most effective way to guarantee that the particular area(s) you are praying for are getting thorough coverage.

Prayer Schedule

A powerful option to help you pray for your leaders is to use a prayer schedule (see Chapter 14 & 15). Organizing your prayers in this way aids you in praying more efficiently. Keep in mind that you do not have to adhere to a strict schedule.

You may choose to develop a guide that is conducive to the demands of your own schedule.

Topical Prayers

In keeping with developing an effective prayer strategy, I have created 15 topical prayers to help you as you seek God on behalf of your leaders. I originally created these in a written document for my prayer partners at the beginning of my itinerate ministry. I believe it is important for you to read through these topical prayers thoroughly before praying for you leader. As you do, it will stir a powerful conviction in your spirit to the needs that your leaders have and to the harsh challenges that they face. If you know what to pray for you will be able to wage effective warfare and witness the evidence that you prayers are being answered.

These topical prayers have been tried and true in my life over the years and have helped my prayer partners effectively pray for my family, my ministry and me. I cannot tell you the manifold blessings that have resulted from these prayers. Therefore, I have provided them for you to use as a guide to praying for your leaders as well. As you pray through these following topical prayers, it is critical to be led of by the Holy Spirit. These written prayers serve as a catalyst for God's words to flow through you as you pray.

In the following topical prayers, I have provided blanks for you to fill in the name for the leader God has led you to pray for. Although these prayers are male gender specific, you may also make them female specific as well. Also, I give you full permission to copy as many pages of these prayers as your prayer partner list allows.

1. Family

Heavenly Father, thank you for covering _____'s children (Names of children). Shield them from all danger of the enemy. We break any demonic assignment set against them. As _____ ministers at home and abroad, grant his family safety and peace. We plead the blood of Jesus on their property and may blessings flow and curses flee from the four walls of their home. Let the windows of Heaven be opened above them and the River of God flow mightily beneath them. May they prosper and be in health even as their soul prospers.

As _____ ministers, speak into the hearts of the whole family and let them see the commitment that he is making to God. At the same time give _____ quality time with to invest into the lives of his children and be the parent you have called him to be even in his unique ministry calling. As _____ sows obedience to God, may the fruit of righteousness and sensitivity to the will of God grow abundantly in the children's hearts. Place within them a passion for the things of God and may Your hand be dynamically evident upon them.

Give _____'s wife/husband supernatural emotional, physical and mental strength as he faces the everyday challenges and pressures while on assignment. Grant him the necessary wisdom in caring for the home and children. Help him to be at peace as the unexpected occurs and to overcome any fears that may accompany any complicated stress. We ask that _____ will be able to accompany _____ on as many ministry assignments as possible and that there will be adequate and appropriate childcare available. When people cross the threshold of their doors, let them encounter the residue of God's presence.

Thank You Father that _____'s marriage is a model of a strong and Godly marriage. Never let the two of them grow distant in their relationship the rigors of ministry responsibilities. Create an indestructible barrier of unity between them and help them to maintain constant and clear communication in every area of their lives. Provide ample opportunities for love, romance, intimacy and true friendship in their relationship.

2. Results

Thank you God for making _____ more desperate to see souls come into the Kingdom of God. May he see tangible results in the form of numerous salvations, conversion, healings, miracles and Holy Spirit baptisms. Break the yoke of bondage off of people's lives through him ministry. May _____ demonstrate a spirit of might and power for we know it is not by his might, nor by his power but by the mighty Holy Spirit working through him. _____'s ministry is about what You do through his ministry. As _____ makes this ministry about You we know You will make his way prosperous and grant much success. Let _____'s heart beat with the things that make Your heart beat and may he be in total sync with your purposes. May he return joyfully from each event bringing with him a basket full of fruit from the harvest, reaping bountifully for the glory of Your kingdom.

3. Glory

Lord, cause _____ to prioritize the importance of Your revealed glory in Christ, the supernatural anointing to do the works of Jesus and your manifest presence in every ministry assignment. Awaken a within him a desire for a greater awareness of Your presence in his personal times of worship. Cause him to be in private what he professes in public. Awaken in those who receive his ministry a double portion of glory and may his passion for You be contagious. May he inspire true Godly vision in people's hearts and empower them to receive it and walk it out in their everyday lives.

4. Protection

We bind and break any attempt by the enemy to cause division, misunderstanding and confusion in _____'s family, ministry team and relationships. Cause all hate, envy, jealousy and lies to be silenced. Protect his reputation from false accusation. Cause your truth and justice to always go before him and shine as the noonday sun in his defense. Destroy opposition and break every snare that has been set before him. Deliver _____ from demonic ambush and cause even his enemies to be at peace with him. Help him fearlessly and faithfully carry his assignments. Cause him to walk in Godly diplomacy as he build bridges of trust and yet not be swayed by the fear of man.

5. Integrity

Lord blanket _____'s integrity and moral character. Do not allow him to go the way of other fallen ministers. Cause him to never lose one shred of his influence. We know he is a threat to the enemy and thus has become a primary target for demonic attack. Cause him to slip under the enemy's radar so as to go unnoticed by his evil schemes yet grant him the boldness to be fearless regarding the roar of the enemy. We are not ignorant of satan's schemes. Help him refuse to accept a false sense of security in his own righteousness and help him to establish solid safety systems of accountability around his family and ministry. Help _____ demonstrate the highest level of faithful stewardship over all the resources You entrust to him. Help him to be fully prepared for the promotion, abundance, and increase that is surely coming his way.

The overwhelming nature of his circumstances is a sign that You truly are directing him and You are the initiator and sustainer of his task. Therefore, send a spirit of fresh faith for the assignment You have given him. Give precise clarity so that he will not succumb to discouragement and second-guessing. Empower him to persevere through hardship, storm and discouragement. When he is weakened by an absence of results in the natural realm help him to never lose sight of Your precious promises for his life and ministry. Empower him to run with optimism and never allow his attitude to cast a shadow on his future. Help him to always have a vision of the goal so that he may pass through every process with confidence, not shrinking back at Your promises

7. Focus

God of all Grace, create a passion within _____ to prioritize the presence of God wherever You send him. Help him to stay true and never veer from your vision for him life. Fan the flame of your presence within him. There is nothing more important than your presence and anointing. Make Leviticus 6:9-13 a primary mandate to for the flame of God's presence to burn furiously in his life. There will be many opportunities for _____ to add more to his plate than what God has given. Lord, do not let winds, rains or storms to put out the fire of passion in his heart

8. Provision

Father of all abundance, we ask that you supply all of _____'s family and ministry's needs according to your riches in Glory. Give him pro-vision for the-vision. Help him to clearly understand what it is you are assigning him to do so he will wisely seek out and invest resources according to that assignment. We are confident as we pray that you are hearing us and releasing kingdom provision for the vision. Supply _____ with all the promotional products that truly bring honor to God and not his own kingdom. At the same time provide him with the necessary income to provide for his family as you have given all things for them to enjoy. We know that _____ has and continues to sacrificially give much of his own personal income to the advancing of the Kingdom of God. Therefore, according to Your great and exceedingly precious promises, we pray a hundred-fold increase on all his investments into Your Kingdom. May every sacrifice of his own resources tumble back into his life in waves of increase.

9. Wisdom

Heavenly Father, grant _____ supernatural wisdom that supersedes the wisdom and methods of man. Help him to recognize Your hand in his life even if it seems to be contrary to natural convention. Keep him from running ahead of Your divine purposes for his life. Help him to resist being involved in activities and opportunities that Your Spirit hasn't endorsed. Help him to exercise patience in stepping out into uncharted territory. Grant him strong discernment when making critical decisions involving relationships, finances, and ministry opportunities. Keep a guard over his mouth as to preserve sound discretion and help him keep a safe distance from potentially harmful vices that would destroy his integrity and mar the pure motivation of his intentions.

10. Expansion

Heavenly Father, we thank you for allowing _____ to be in position of uncertainty at various times as it will help him keep focused and dependent on You. Supernaturally create open doors of ministry opportunity where he will have the greatest impact. Keep his schedule full of appointments only to the degree that he and his family can handle at each stage of ministry development. Ordain his steps and put him in front of the right people that lead to Godly opportunities. Don't allow him to seek *good* opportunities, but rather *God* opportunities. Help him stand watch that he will not enter into distractions that will lure him away from Your vision and purpose. Also, open doors for ministry in foreign missions and grant the provision for him to walk through them.

11. Creativity

Remove all hindrances to creativity within _____ and inspire within him powerful and anointed ministry methods from Heaven accompanied by a fresh sound that flows from Your throne. Help him to be a receiver of Your creativity and to release that creativity in holy unction. May the sound of Heaven resound from his heart and help him innovatively and creatively draw this generation into Your presence. Grant him the creative solutions to problems that arise in his ministry and help him to rely upon your strength instead of his own ability. Bring creative and administrative people into _____'s life to absorb the responsibilities of things that would distract him from his creative focus: to pray, study the Word of God and minister. Help him not to get caught up in minute details that bog him down and smother Your creative flow within him. Grant to him all the necessary resources in the media arts to effectively minister with excellence.

12. Connections

Connect _____ to God's leading men and women in ministry who are on the cutting edge of what you are doing in the earth. May he be linked with God's generals in ministry, politics and government around the world. As his ministry grows help him to focus his prayers, finances and main efforts into each season of development. Give him prophetic insight so he will not chase after those individuals who are concerned with a worldly quest for promotion. Rather, we seek Your extreme favor with connections for the purpose of widespread exposure of the passion God has placed in him: to uncompromisingly declare the gospel of Jesus Christ. This includes necessary partnerships to powerful ministries that are on the cusp of what You are truly doing. Give him relationships to help him stay accountable in every area of his life. Keep _____ from submitting any of his gifts and future to anyone who has selfish agendas for his life. Help him to realize that there are those who would seek to master him as a subject in their own kingdoms and drain valuable anointing and energy from his spirit. Help him stay aware of the enemy's vices in this area and keep his ambitions covered in the blood and nailed to the cross.

13. Prayer Life

Heavenly Father, help _____ to diligently maintain his commitment to Your passion for his prayer life. Protect his times of intimacy and intercession so as not to lose power, purpose and priority. Help him to not grow weary in this area, for it is the life breath of the ministry. Help us as his intercessors as we cover him in prayer to have clear discernment in any areas that would weaken and distract him from the critical nature of his relationship with You. For it is in the burning bush experiences of his life that his power, anointing, strategy, vision and assignment for his life will flow. Inspire him toward living life in the center of private worship and intercession. As he shows up for You in private, we ask that you show up for him in public arenas of ministry and confirm Your mighty hand in his life so lives will be transformed.

15. Appointments

We pray over each appointment on _____'s itinerary and declare total victory and success over every administrative detail. We ask that you prepare the ground ahead of time and work in the hearts of those who will receive from his ministry. Grant glorious victory before each campaign and set the stage for the miraculous. Give him keen prophetic insight in how to pray and minister in each area. Reveal strongholds, principalities and demonic dominions that are hindering a breakthrough in each event and provide key strategies to casting down everything that exalts itself against the knowledge of God. Thank you for granting _____ full permission and unlimited access to the Heavenly resources and kingdom connections. In every favorable opportunity enable him to authorize and establish the Kingdom of God as being superior to the kingdom of darkness. Allow him to be unhindered in his progress and unstoppable in Your mission for his life and ministry.

Let worship and intercession rise to a higher level and greater intensity than ever before and rain down holy fire on each gathering that _____ is a part of or in direct leadership over. Grant favor and agreement with key leaders he connects with in each church, province, city and territory, and cause long lasting kingdom and covenant relationships to form. Let Your Spirit lead him to connect with key ministry and civic leaders to help establish change in politics and public policies. Give him supernatural leadership ability and powerful influence as to create environments that establish justice, peace and God's presence in the earth.

Chapter 7

PRAYER PARTNERSHIP

"So David waxed greater and greater: for the LORD of hosts was with him." ~ **1 Chronicles 11:9 KJV**

King David had thirty mighty men in whom he depended on for everything. Among them were three men in particular who by their stoic acts of bravery, attained extraordinary victories for their king. Their stories are quite astonishing. With only a spear in his hand, Adino the Eznite wreaked havoc on 800 men at one time. Jashobeam, the chief of the captains, took down 300 men at once, again only with a spear. Eleazar the Adhohite captured an entire barley field that was strewn out with a battalion of Philistines single handedly with a sword. Astounding! These mighty men are also recorded to have slain four giants as big as Goliath (2 Samuel 21:15-22). The book of 2 Chronicles 11 tells us that these three men broke through a garrison of Philistines just to bring him back a canteen of water. What ferocity! Our key passage above tells us that David had consistent and credible victories and these accounts of his champion campaigns spread to the enemies who would dare oppose him. Note that this passage comes right before the record of some of the most valiant deeds of his mighty protectors. Oh what victories our ministers and leaders would have if only they were surrounded by mighty men. How many mighty men does your pastor or leader have? Are you one of them; one who will stand in the gap for him and help him slay giants of wickedness that are posed against him? Or are you one to join forces with the enemies pitted against him through slander, criticism, gossip and maligning?

The word *intercessor* in Hebrew is *paga,* which is a military term meaning to take position at the flank between the enemy and the one being assailed and stand him off in full rear assault. It's a defensive term that implies protecting from all sides, especially behind the back (which is where most spiritual attacks originate). As potential prayer partners for ministries, we must understand that satan's anger isn't quenched from our past victories. From the rear flanks of defeat, he is yet scheming from the day of his demise to bring retribution upon men and women of God at a later time when they least expect it (1 peter 5:7).

I once heard of sign in a local police station's weight room that read, *"The prisoners at the state penitentiary are pumping iron... You better be pumping iron too."* The devil doesn't sit idly back while ministers are preparing their lives and ministries to advance the kingdom of God and establish its supremacy in the earth.

One thing is absolutely certain: churches, ministries and missionaries must enlist committed prayer partners to cover the mighty men and women of God that are focused on seeing God's Kingdom established on the earth. In a battle against the Amelekites, the children of Israel under Joshua's charge and Moses' command, gained strong advantage over the enemy and ultimately sustained victory as long as Moses stood with his hands raised, holding out his staff. However, when Moses' hands fell from weariness the Israelites would be forced into retreat and would lose ground in the war. It was only when Aaron and Hur held Moses' hands up that the Israelites were able to rout the Amelekites into defeat.

"Joshua did as Moses told him, and fought against Amalek; and Moses, Aaron, and Hur went up to the top of the hill. So it came about when Moses held his hand up, that Israel prevailed, and when he let his hand down, Amalek prevailed. But Moses' hands were heavy. Then they took a stone and put it under him, and he sat on it; and Aaron and Hur supported his hands, one on one side and one on the other. Thus his hands were steady until the sun set. So Joshua overwhelmed Amalek and his people with the edge of the sword." ~ **Exodus 17:10-13**

Aaron and Hur represent the prayer warriors that help to hold up the hands of ministers who are flailing in the work of the Lord. Where are the Aarons and the Hurs of our generation? Oh the battles that have been lost because there was no one to hold up the hands of the generals of the faith who have become weary from the fight.

Becoming an Effective Prayer Partner

The following are practical ways in which you can support your leaders through the ministry of intercession:

1. Pray for your leaders without the need to be recognized by them. If you can do this without the need for their approval you will make the ideal prayer partner. Too many people want to be the "prayer partner" for their leader in order to be brought under their wing or become a groupie. These types of people can be sifted quickly by discerning leadership and completely ingnored. Many want to serve as ring leaders for ministry because of the title. Don't be title conscious. Be sincerely servant conscious and God will open doors for your prayer ministry.

2. Occasionally (emphasis on occasionally) contact the ministers you pray for by phone. If you reach their voice mail, leave a message (without obligating them to return the call). You can also send a text, which is often the desired option amongst busy ministers. Respect their time and don't use the prayer ministry as a way to get "in roads" towards a close relationship. You don't have to be close to the leaders you pray for to see significant results. You don't want your leader to grow weary of you but to appreciate and have a desire to call on you as needed.

3. If you have a "word" from God or a heavy warning, be sensitive as to whether or not it should be shared or discreetly prayed for privately.

4. If you have a dream or a vision for the minister and his family, ask the Lord for the interpretation. If you are not sure that something you are receiving is from the Lord, take more time to pray until you get a sure release and then share it with an open heart. Always start your exhortation with *"I think I hear the Lord saying"* or *"I submit this to you for your consideration."* When you start your word of with *"Thus says the Lord..."* you make it difficult for the leader to process it. Offer your insights gently and humbly. If God rejects the proud then most likely so will your leader.

5. It may take time to build trust in the validity of your ministry of intercession. Be faithful in your praying and wait for the relationship to form as the Lord wills.

6. Ministers need to know they are being prayed for. This encourages them and strengthens their resolve to continue through the difficult times. Therefore, try to offer feedback on a regular basis on what the Lord is telling you. Simply sending a text message or a brief email is all a leader often needs to regain momentary strength.

7. Seek to gain access with your leader through appropriate correspondence. Be sure to ask them if you can connect with them by email. Also, letters and faxes are

an option for effective communication. Sometimes a short text-message can offer great comfort and encouragement without draining time from your leader. Remember, they have a very demanding schedule and rather than exhaust them with a long rhetorical, prophetic & poetic word or prayer, you can actually energize and empower them with a short blast for the moments ahead. The goal is to motivate them by faith and encouragement. Bombarding them will actually backfire and will cause them to deny or reject the prayer insight you offer.

8. Ministers especially need your prayers the day/night before they minister and the season of time directly following. These are times when distractions and mental pressures enter a leader's mind. Emotional stress is particularly prevalent. It is not uncommon for family problems, particularly in the marriage and with the children to come under attack. When a minister's spouse is struggling it brings tension to the whole marriage. As the old adage goes, *"Happy Wife, happy life."* Therefore, when you pray specifically target these areas that the peace of God may rule in every situation directly connected to the family unit.

Satan is full of jealousy, anger and fear over the things God is about to do or has already done through His select vessels. According to many influential ministers, the day before and after ministry is when leaders most fight depression, criticism and disappointment and therefore most need prayer (See Matthew 4:11). It has been said that two hours of ministry is like an eight-hour workday for most. This is due to the spiritual warfare involved. It is not unusual for itinerate ministers to experience emotional, physical and spiritual exhaustion for several days following ventures abroad. It is even very common for them to face financial setbacks for a season. Is it any wonder why Paul said, *"Fight the good fight of faith."* (1 Timothy 6:12)

Your prayers are crucial for the full recovery of your leaders. They will be extremely grateful to know you are covering them regarding these most sensitive areas of their lives. A note of caution: since you have been assigned to pray for the needs of your leader it would be wise to pray for yourself and your family as well. We must be aware of Satan's strategy. If he fails at one assault he will try another. If he can take down prayer ministries designed to cover leaders then he will have greater access to leadership. Don't be fooled. Be sober and vigilant. Also, remember that praying for the ministry should never replace your own prayer time with God. Being in God's network of intercessors requires extra time on your part and is a sacrifice of love.

The Prayer Partner's Personal Preparation

As a prayer partner, it is important that you prepare your heart before launching into the battle. Here are some ways you can prepare your heart for intercession:

1. Be Still – Calming your mind and emptying thoughts of frustration and irritation positions you to see and hear from God clearly. When you have a clear picture of God you will understand His heart and willingness to answer your prayers. Being still also gives God the chance to speak first. (Psalms 46:10).

2. Calm Down – It is important to trust God regarding dilemmas, struggles, and fears from the moment you begin intercessory prayer in order to effectively pray. Come boldly proclaiming the peace of God over your situation and enter the presence of God with confidence (1 Peter 5:7).

3. Give Thanks – A complaining spirit will hinder your prayers. Having a grateful heart ignites our faith and helps us have clearer focus. Through thanks, we are already proclaiming what we have before we see it (Hebrews 11:1). This is why God tells us to enter His presence with thanksgiving (Psalms 100:4). Praise naturally flows from a thankful heart.

4. Worship First – Jesus taught His disciples that worship was the priority of prayer (Luke 11:2). That's why He told them to first address God as their Father. Our Heavenly Father never judges us according to our successes or failures but on the success of Jesus. Entering into intimacy with God as Father helps us focus on His ability not our ability. Through worship we are lifted from the temporal into the eternal; where imagination, creativity and impossibilities are seen as possibilities. We access the heart of God through worship. Here is something else to think about: The word 'ear' is the middle of the word Heart. When we worship we speak the language of God's heart and He always listens most intently to the 'heart-cry.'"

5. Receive Grace – Condemnation keeps us from praying confidently. Therefore, we must receive God's Grace when we pray. We do not present our pleas because of our righteousness but because of God's great mercy (Daniel 9:18). We will most certainly not have all our issues worked out but we must know that we are acceptable to God based on His righteousness and not our own. God doesn't come through for us because we are faithful. He comes through for us because HE is faithful. Our fervent prayers should not be based on our good performance but Christ's good performance. I highly recommend you to read my foundational book entitled GRACEWORKS to further understand your position in Christ through the New Covenant of Grace. This revelation will fuel your fire for fervent and effective praying. (Romans 8:1).

6. Give Grace – An unforgiving heart keeps us from hearing from God and unclear as to how much He loves us. Grace is directly linked to forgiveness and forgiveness is directly linked to mountains being moved (Job 42:10; Mark 11:23-25; Luke 11:3-4). Also, when we harbor bitter grudges against others it hurts us more than the offender. However, when we release forgiveness a flood of God's love will surge through us towards our enemies. It is hard to be angry with someone for very long when we are praying for them. Our prayers are unhindered when we forgive (Matthew 5:24). Prayer also releases love even toward those who have wounded us. Forgiveness helps us to love like we've never been hurt.

7. Rest Secure – Knowing you are invincible in the armor of Christ's righteousness gives great strength. In fact resting in Christ doesn't cause us to fall asleep. It makes us more alert and aware than ever. We rest in Christ's Identity that we may pray with Christ's fervency. When we're secure in our identity in Christ we do not pray with selfish motives. Our prayers will be for the best interests of others when we know who we are in Christ. When we finally realize we are completely covered in Christ we can pray in His power and not our own. Arm yourself with this truth (Ephesians 6:10-20).

Conclusion: Your leaders desperately need you. Your prayers hold the power to bend the rulers of this age and bring the authority of Heaven down to change the course of history on planet Earth. Becoming a prayer partner enables you to become a prayer missionary as you pray for the ministries that represent Jesus worldwide Your prayers actually travel around the globe enforcing the Kingdom of God and enacting a demonstration of His mighty power.

Chapter 8

THE LEADER'S PRAYER LIFE

"Prayerless men have never been used of God."
~ E. M. Bounds

Attention spiritual leader! These next two chapters are possibly the most important chapters in this book. If you don't know it by now, this book is as crucial for you to read as it is for those whom you lead (readers are leaders). In order to raise others up to pray for you, you must be a leader in prayer yourself. You must have the integrity to be consistent in prayer and be doing all you can in your private prayer life before you muster others to pray on your behalf (I address the subject of developing a personal prayer team in the next chapter).

*"Apostasy generally begins at the closet door." ~ **Philip Henry***

If you do not have a personal prayer life then you must start to develop one. You may say, *"I have lost the feeling to pray."*

Ministry leader: you must pray even when you don't feel like it or else pray UNTIL you feel like it. No more excuses! You cannot continue in the ministry without a dedicated prayer walk. I shouldn't have to say this to spiritual leaders but unfortunately it bears repeating: Leaders amount to nothing in the ministry unless they pray. Pastor and leader, you must be on the alert that the enemy has a plan to destroy your family, your ministry and your very life. That is why you must awaken to the fullness of your calling! If it is possible for a little while, turn off your cell phone, unplug the computer, hide the remote to the television and even cancel your Thursday morning 'T' time at the country club! Please, hear the Holy Spirit! Now it is important for me to insert here that to be a leader in prayer doesn't mean you have to be the best 'pray-er' in the church. However, it does mean that you should make praying a priority in your life.

"Leaders must be released from the idea that they have to be great prayer warriors before they can begin to call others to prayer." ~ **David Bryant**

The point being is that as leaders we are absolutely powerless against the enemy and useless to God unless we are committed to consistent and fervent prayer. The key here being "consistent and fervent." Some leaders feel they are not great men and women of prayer. It isn't the eloquence of our prayer that makes us great. What makes us great prayer disciples in the eyes of God is that we are obedient to pray. If we are simply faithful to pray, we will see tangible results.

"A prayerless ministry is the undertaker for all God's truth and for God's church." ~ **E.M. Bounds**

Leader, please hear me well: you cannot escape the absolute inextricable necessity to pray. Truth is, you cannot stumble while on your knees. Either a leader goes down on his knees or he just goes down. Whatever you are in your life and ministry is the sum total of your prayer life. While Grace will get you to Heaven, prayer will connect you to Heaven's power for your assignment here on earth! We are saved only by Grace but we are empowered when we plug into the source of our salvation. And whether we want to admit it or not our prayer life will ultimately determine our success or failure. How can we think to talk to men if we haven't learned how to talk to God. Friend, if you remember anything you read in this book understand that prayer is THE work of the ministry. Everything else is the fruit of the abundance or the lack thereof. We don't pray so the ministry will work. Ministry 'works' because we pray.

Prayer is the engine in which all ministry activity runs. Without prayer, the minister and his ministry will ultimately fail to reach their fullest potential. Ministry is grueling. Many who have not experienced what the ministry is like will never know what I am talking about. Once, in my 20's, while I was serving as a youth pastor of a very large church in the Southeast United States, I was in my office into the late hours of the night, preparing for a youth service the following evening. While I was sitting in my desk busy clicking away at my computer the church janitor came into my office to clean. As soon as he saw me sitting there he struck up a conversation with me (I was in no mood to talk as I was in a hurry to finish up planning for the next day's youth meeting). His accent immediately clued me in that he was from the Caribbean Islands. His name was Godfrey and God had sent him to into my office to change my life forever. As he observed me frantically fluttering through my Bible and study notes, he immediately asked me, *"Hey man of God; do you have a prayer life."* His question hit me like a spear right through my chest. You see; I had let the business of my ministry overtake my prayer life. While I sat there I felt weakened by my own pride. I sadly and ashamedly answered Godfrey, *"No! I don't!"* He emphatically raised his voice and spoke with spiritual authority, *"What in the world are you doing ministering here, in THIS church without a prayer life? This church will chew you up and spit you out if you don't learn to pray!"*

"A pulpit without a prayer closet will always be a barren thing." ~ **E.M. Bounds**

I began to weep under the power of God as he asked me if he could lay hands on me and pray for me. I agreed, and as he gripped my shoulders with great strength and began to pray like a spiritual giant, I willingly allowed the Holy Spirit to awaken me. After he prayed for me, I sat pinned to my chair under the power of God while he finished cleaning my room and quietly slipped out of my office unnoticed. After that night I never saw him again but I assure you I will never forget him. For it was on that night that the Holy Spirit fully ignited a unquenchable desire to seek the Lord in prayer. Those moments with Godfrey have impacted my life to this very day. I was deeply convicted of my desperate need and marvelous privilege to convene with God and I've never been the same. In my many years as a ministry leader I have learned (unfortunately many times the hard way) that without prayer, ministry would have consumed me. This Biblical account illustrates what happens to a minister who tries to hold up the ministry in his own strength.

"But when they came to the threshing floor of Nacon, Uzzah reached out toward the ark of God and took hold of it, for the oxen nearly upset it. And the anger of the LORD burned against Uzzah, and God struck him down there for his irreverence; and he died there by the ark of God."
~ 2 Samuel 6:6-7 NASB

Uzzah is no different than many of our leaders today. Some ministers try to hold up the ministry (a sacred thing) in their own abilities. As a result, many leaders today have abandoned the call of God all together to deliver pizza, sell cars or launch out blindly into business ventures that have nothing to do with God or His purposes for their lives. This ought not to be. God never intended you to run out of you. All of Heaven's resources are available to you if you would simply learn to pull them down through fervent, diligent and consistent prayer. We literally can command the Heavens to our bidding at God's purposes.

"Thus saith the LORD, the Holy One of Israel, and his Maker, ask me of things to come concerning my sons, and concerning the work of my hands COMMAND YE ME!"
~ Isaiah 45:11 KJV

Starting the Day with Prayer

D.L. Moody once confessed that he felt guilty if he heard the blacksmiths pounding in the morning before he prayed. Great praying is the foundation of all great preaching. I firmly believe that if our day is hemmed in with prayer, it is less likely to come unraveled. For me, the best time of day to pray is the early morning hours. My mind is still and it is quiet and so is everyone else. The latter is the greater part of that equation. Why? Because no one is requiring of me, pressuring me, draining me, demanding of me. I am able to hear God speak to my soul with out interruption. I'll turn the lamp on, prepar a cup of coffee, sit in my favorite chair, open my bible, and beging to read my daily portion. I call it, getting my daily bread. It is my favorite time of the day.

The Bible tells us to be still and then we can have calm assurance that God is in control (Psalms 96:10). In the morning, prayer is the key that opens to us the treasures of God's mercies. In the evening it is the key that shuts us up under his protection and safeguard. Starting the day without prayer and quiet reflection in God's word is in essence saying that we are sufficient enough within ourselves to begin our day and handle the stress and strain that eventually will come. The priority of prayer must be the benchmark of a spiritual leader's life. And if leaders don't stand on top of the hill, someone else will.

"Man is never so tall as when he kneels before God and never so great as when he humbles himself before God. And the man who kneels to God can stand up to anything."
~ Louis H. Evans

For many leaders (and most of us for that matter) the listening process usually starts as soon as we wake up. From the moment the alarm clock goes off the listening begins. However, rather than stumble through our morning routine, we must direct the thoughts in our mind instead of simply being at their mercy. Often we entertain complains about that happened yesterday or worries about what's coming today. Instead, we need to immediately take charge of our thinking at the onset of each sunrise. We can declare war on fear, doubt, and depression by speaking the truth to ourselves and set the right tone by mentally affirming our dependence upon God and our need for Him. Leaders should not get on the horse of each day without first grabbing the reigns properly. King David was one for rising early to seek God. As a leader myself I want to be mentored by God's favorite leaders in scripture. Therefore, I follow David's example and wake up my day rather than let my day wake me up.

"In the morning, O LORD, You will hear my voice; in the morning I will order my prayer to You and eagerly watch."
~ Psalms 5:3 NASB

The Hebrew word for 'direct' is *'arak'* which means *battle strategy*. In other words, each morning as David prayed he was able to seek the Lord and get God's strategy for the many battles that he fought and won. We as leaders would do well to do the same. Leaders must learn to submit their plans to God and listen to the Holy Spirit's instructions for each day

"There is something about the morning that awakens the God who never sleeps nor slumbers. Yes, something about the dawn that causes our God to "arise" all through our history. In the scriptures, we find that God loves the morning. He loves meeting His people and displaying His glory and greatness in the morning." ~ **Chris Tomlin**

How can we begin anything without God's counsel? I believe that far too often we as leaders have the tendency to charge into our day motivated by self sufficiency. When I start my day I must hear what God has to say before I hear what anybody else has to say. When we start our day with God we properly strategize and prioritize our day. If we say we put God first then we must walk it out in practicality. Therefore, starting our day with God testifies that we put God first everyday. There will be times when we aren't able to start each day with God. It is when it becomes habitual that we compromise our wall and allow for breaches to occur. The way we start our day is the way we usually walk through it and finish it. When we start our day with God we properly cultivate the way we respond to the challenges that face us.

"How we begin our morning so often sets the tone for the day... The most decisive time of our day is very often our first waking moments, because they color everything to come... Begin your day by acknowledging your dependence upon God and your need for God. Purpose by Grace that your first thought of the day will be an expression of your dependence on God, your need for God, and your confidence in God. Sin, including especially the sin of pride, is active, not passive. Sin doesn't wake up tired, because it hasn't been sleeping. When you wake up in the morning, sin is right there, fully awake, ready to attack. So rather than be attacked by sin in the morning, I've chosen to go on the offensive.... From the moment I'm awake, I've learned to make statements to God about my dependence upon God, and in this way I'm humbling myself before God" ~ **C.J. Mahaney**

For Further study on seeking God in the morning:

Genesis 22:3; 28:18; Exodus 16:21; 24:4 30:7-8; 32:1; 34:2-4; Joshua 3:1; 6:12,15,20; 7:16; 8:10; Judges 9:33; Psalms 30:5; 57:8; 59:16; 90:14; 101:8; 108:2; 119:147; Psalms 63:1; Psalms 139:9; Proverbs 8:17; 23:21; 24:33-34; Isaiah 9:2; 26:9; 40:4; Isaiah 40:30-31; Jeremiah 7:13, 25; 11:7; 26:5; Lamentations 3:22-23; Hosea 6:3-4; 1 Samuel 15:12; Matthew 14:25; Matthew 25:5; Mark 1:35; 16:2; Ephesians 5:14; 1 Thessalonians 5:6-8

Don't be a Night Owl

God never requires sleep, but we do! Therefore, I thought it important to make a few remarks regarding the importance of sleep in the life of the believer. After all, if we plan to seek God early in the morning then we must evaluate our sleep patterns and properly plan how we end each day.

"For you are all sons of light and sons of day. We are not of night nor of darkness." ~ **1 Thessalonians 5:5**

There was a very popular song several years ago called *The Freaks Come Out at Night.* This is true in the real sense. I believe demonic activity is most prevalent in the late hours of the night. One can observe in our sinful culture that it is the night hours when most violent crimes and deviant behaviors occur. The Bible also seems to support the fact that it is the late hours of the night where the enemy is most at work (See Genesis 19:35; Exodus 12:12; 1 Samuel 28:8; Job 27:20; Psalms 55:10; Psalms 91:5; Song of Songs 3:8; Obadiah 1:5; John 11:10; 1 Thessalonians 5:2).

I'll be the first to admit that I enjoy staying up late at night; I always have. I can remember from the time I was a young child I resisted bedtime. Even now, I'm somewhat of a "night owl" when it comes to my lifestyle and I constantly have to resist my tendency and the temptation to stay up late. I know that if I'm going to be any earthly good for my family, my ministry and for others then I have to discipline myself and surrender my will to God's purpose for sleep in my life (and that means surrender early).

"The night is almost gone, and the day is near. Therefore let us lay aside the deeds of darkness and put on the armor of light.

Let us behave properly as in the day, not in carousing and drunkenness, not in sexual promiscuity and sensuality, not in strife and jealousy. But put on the Lord Jesus Christ, and make no provision for the flesh in regard to its lusts."
~ Romans 13:12-13 NASB

"Do not long for the night, when people vanish in their place. "Be careful, do not turn to evil..." **~ Job 36:20-21 NASB**

called melatonin that aids in the relaxation of the body. When we fight sleep we are fighting against God's creative order. This is a form of pride. When we stay up too late we are saying that we are sufficient enough to sustain ourselves past God's created limitations. When we cross over God's boundaries for our physical bodies we run past what our make-up is designed to handle.

The way we end today can clearly affect the way we encounter tomorrow. When we are tired it is a reminder that we are undone without God's sustaining Grace. As we sleep through the night, our strength is restored, our body recovers, our mind is renewed, and we're refreshed to live for God and experience His mercies for the next day. God created the need for restful sleep within each of us and there's a spiritual reason for it. Each night as our body and mind is depleted of strength we are reminded that we are dependent creatures. We are not self-sufficient. When we accept the pattern of sleep God designed for us we humble ourselves before Him and reap the benefits that come along with adequate rest and recovery.

We must do our part as we allow the Holy Spirit to guard our precious hours of sleep. Thus, it is also important to note that we must not allow worry to keep us up at night (Also see Psalms 4:8). This is a scheme of the enemy to rob us of the proper amount of sleep our bodies need. We also must be careful to not aid the enemy and freely hand over the treasure of our rest to him by staying up too late. The enemy works tirelessly (if you will) to keep us physically, mentally, emotionally and spiritual exhausted. If he is successful in his attempts to thwart our rest we become more susceptible to defeat.

"Do not worry about tomorrow; for tomorrow will care for itself." ~ **Matthew 6:34 NASB**

When we fight sleep, we fight God. Wisdom denotes that we should never make important decisions when we are tired. Yet many of us try to solve the world's problems late at night. It is also very popular in the youth culture to stay up late at night (surfing the internet, watching T.V. hanging out with friends, etc.). However, when our bodies are tired our ability to make good life choices is skewed because our judgment is impaired. We must humble ourselves and allow our bodies to recover properly so we will be all God wants us to be for the challenges of the following day. This is not to say that occasionally we will have deadlines that have to be met that require extra time late at night. However, a regular occurrence of lack of sleep will eventually cause us to make wrong decisions, unwise judgments and unnecessary mistakes to the detriment of others and ourselves. A lifestyle of lack of sleep ultimately results in dishonoring God. The end of each day offers us a unique opportunity to cultivate humility and weaken pride, as well as to sense God's pleasure

Dream Escape

Another reason to hit the sack early is because God longs to meet us in our dreams. There He can reveal things we would never perceive while awake. Throughout the Bible God often spoke and revealed Himself in dreams.

"God spoke to Israel in visions of the night and said, "Jacob, Jacob." And he said, "Here I am." ~ **Genesis 46:2 NASB**

"In Gibeon the LORD appeared to Solomon in a dream at night; and God said, "Ask what you wish me to give you."
~ **1 Kings 3:5 NASB**

It is a known fact that our bodies require a certain amount of time within the sleep cycle before we enter 'dream stage.' This is called R.E.M. sleep (rapid eye movement). During this 4th cycle of sleep is where most dreams occur. If we allow enough time for sleep (at least 8 hours) we give God a greater opportunity to speak to us in our sleep in a much more powerful way than when we're awake. In our dreams God can freely enter our subconscious, rekindle our imagination and revive amazing possibilities!

The Secret Place

The secret to praying is praying in secret: pulling away from all the stress and business of our lives to spend quiet, quality time with God. If I were to ask you to show me the place where you spend time with God (your special secret place) could you show it to me? Jesus Himself instructed us to enter our secret place whenever we pray. We should have a secret place.

"When you pray, you are not to be like the hypocrites; for they love to stand and pray in the synagogues and on the street corners so that they may be seen by men. Truly I say to you, they have their reward in full. But you, when you pray, go into your inner room, close your door and pray to your Father who is in secret, and your Father who sees {what is done} in secret will reward you. And when you are praying, do not use meaningless repetition as the Gentiles do, for they suppose that they will be heard for their many words."
~ Matthew 6:5-6 NASB

Note Jesus didn't say, *"IF you pray."* He said, *"WHEN you pray."* As a little boy living with my grandma, I would watch her for hours everyday swiveling back and forth in her red velvet chair in a special room in her house crying tears, singing songs, reading the Word of God and calling out to Him in fervent prayer. Grandma is with Jesus now but her prayers still live on. My parents still have that red prayer chair. Sometimes when I visit my parents I often will slip back into her room and sit in that chair and thank God for the prayers that have kept me to this day. Many times I can feel the presence of God in that chair because of the power of her prayers.

"All ability to talk to men is measured by the ability with which a preacher can talk to God for men. He who ploughs not in his closet, will never reap in his pulpit." ~ **E.M. Bounds**

I have learned a great deal about praying in secret over the years and each day as I stumble into my secret place in the basement of my home, I feel the holy atmosphere that God and I have created together as I worship Him and He speaks words of love into my spirit. I have seen God do incredible things in my life and it is because of the prayers that have been prayed in that secret place. Many times I have anointed the walls of my special place, laid my hands on those walls and prayed these words…

"Blessings flow and curses flee from the four walls of my house. Open the windows of Heaven and pour out a blessing that I cannot contain and may the river of God flow mightily beneath my feet."

Jesus Himself had a secret place. It was usually in the hidden brush of the Mount of Olives where you could find him often fervently seeking His Father's for His purposes and the strength for all that lie ahead for Him. If Jesus prayed in secret, who are we to think that we can foolishly race past the calls of the secret place for our lives.

"But Jesus Himself would often slip away to the wilderness and pray." ~ **Luke 5:16 NASB**

The truth is that all of God's called men and women must lay hold of His power in prayer and pull down the authority of the Kingdom of God as to establish its purpose, and power, its reality and rule in our homes, our churches, our ministries and our governments. Sadly, much of the battles that have been lost were not for lack of speaking ability, talent, creative programming or such the like. Rather countless victories have been freely handed over for the insufficiency of prayer.

Spiritual leader: It is not too late to start praying! Don't let the days that you haven't prayed discourage you from the fruitful days of prayer that lie ahead. Do you have big dreams? Do you have seemingly insurmountable obstacles, impending fears and unsolvable questions? Although you may not have immediate answers to your prayers, there is one sure answer: Prayer! Instead of wandering around in circles you can actually *pray circles* around your dreams, obstacles, fears and questions! And there, God will give clear vision, sure solution and peace beyond understanding for every need and situation that you face. Remember: *You don't get what you want; YOU REPRODUCE WHAT YOU ARE!* If you want to reproduce fervent prayer warriors then be one! The most effective prayers you will ever pray are the ones you pray for yourself. Then *as you pray* you will naturally raise up others to pray *as you pray*. By all means, don't let the prayers of others be a substitute for your own praying. You know yourself better than anyone else!

"Is anyone among you suffering? Then he must pray. Is anyone cheerful? He is to sing praises." ~ **James 5:13 NASB**

God has amazing secrets reserved only for the secret place. God never shouts His secrets, He only whispers them. Don't ignore the gentle promptings of the Holy Spirit to commune with Him in the secret place. When you are sensitive and responsive to His biddings you will unearth glorious treasures waiting to be discovered.

The late and great evangelist Rodney Smith, born in the Epping Forest just on the outskirts of London in 1860, is a powerful example of How God can use a man of humble beginnings to turn his generation upside down. Rodney never received a formal education, yet he lectured at Harvard. He was actually born in a tent in a gypsy commune, yet he was invited to the White House to counsel two presidents. It is said that he actually made the long journey across the Atlantic Ocean some forty-five times to preach the Gospel to literally millions of people in his lifetime. Once a group of men, hungry for revival, approached him and asked him how God could so use them as He was using Smith. Without hesitation he answered...[48]

"Go home, lock yourself in your room. Kneel down in the middle of the floor, and with a piece of chalk draw a circle around yourself. There, on your knees, pray fervently and brokenly that God would start a revival within that chalk circle.'
~ **Rodney "Gypsy" Smith**[48]

Chapter 9

THE LEADER'S PRAYER TEAM

"The minister needs the prayer of his people. He has a right to it. He is in very truth dependent on it. It is his task to train Christians for their work of intercession on behalf of the church and the world. He must begin with training them to pray for himself." ~ **Andrew Murray**

Charles Haddon Spurgeon (1834-1892) was England's best-known preacher for most of the second half of the 19th century. In 1854, just four years after his conversion, Spurgeon, then only 20 years of age, became pastor of London's famed New Park Street Church (formerly pastored by the famous Baptist theologian John Gill). The congregation quickly outgrew their building, moved to Exeter Hall, then to Surrey Music Hall. In these venues Spurgeon frequently preached to audiences numbering more than 10,000—all in the days before electronic amplification. In 1861 the congregation moved permanently to the newly

131

constructed Metropolitan Tabernacle. Once during a revival meeting under Spurgeon's preaching, D.L. Moody (who had attended) asked Spurgeon to tell him the secret of the mass salvations. Spurgeon simply responded by pointing down to the floor. Perplexed Moody asked what this meant. Spurgeon replied by saying that each night while he was preaching there were at least 100 fervent prayer warriors interceding for him in a room directly under the platform. Prayer was the secret of Spurgeon's evangelistic power!

"Leaders must develop an early warning system if we expect to survive. You must develop a watchful team of intercessors who are committed to praying for you. Those whose ministries are crashing and burning today most likely ignored prophetic council from people who saw disaster coming their way."
~ J. Lee Grady

Having a fervent team of intercessors is like having your own built-in early warning system. They can assist you in keeping keen discernment in your ministry. When a pastor or leader does not give diligent attention to the strong administration and prayer as the central core of their ministry, it is like attempting to start a fire in the fireplace without the kindling and the wood. Therefore, it is imperative that a pastor chooses and empowers loyal prayer team leaders who love him and know his heart to further build and lead his prayer ministry. If a leader chooses to allow someone else, outside of his direct sphere of influence, to build a prayer team for his ministry he is opening the door to many problems. Pastors should take full responsibility for developing their own prayer coverage. If you are called to scale the heights of greatness in God and His purposes for your life, then you must decide now that it is no longer an option for you to neglect developing a solid prayer covering over your life. No one else is going to do it for you like you will do it for you.

"The price of greatness is responsibility." ~ **Winston Churchill**

Taking ownership of raising up a personal prayer team by choosing and empowering leaders who share your heart for the ministry can seem time consuming. After all, pastors have enough on their plate already. However, have you stopped to consider how many activities in your schedule are those in which you've initiated outside of God's direction? In other words, what things on your itinerary could be considered more important than raising up a prayer team? This is a question you must ask yourself. Considering this will help you to eliminate the possible distractions and unnecessary items from your agenda.

Much of the lack of progress and effectiveness in the church is due to the anemic state of our local church prayer agencies. Just think; you could be standing high on the shoulders of those whom you raise up to pray for you. That's the paradox of building a personal prayer team. As you raise *them* up, they raise *you* up.

"The potency of prayer hath subdued the strength of fire; it hath bridled the rage of lions hushed anarchy to rest, extinguished wars, appeased the elements, expelled demons,

burst the chains of death, expanded the gates Heaven, assuaged diseases, repelled frauds, rescued cities from destruction, stayed the sun in its course, and arrested the progress of the thunderbolt. Prayer is all-efficient panoply, a treasure undiminished, a mine, which is never exhausted, a sky unobscured by clouds, a Heaven unruffled by the storm. It is the root, the fountain, the mother of a thousand blessings."
~ John Chrysostom

During the darkest hour of His life, even Jesus our Lord asked His disciples to "keep watch" (pray) with Him. If Jesus asked those closest to Him to pray for Him, the spiritual leader must also take strong measures to request the same fervency of His prayer team.

"Then Jesus came with them to a place called Gethsemane, and said to His disciples, 'Sit here while I go over there and pray.' And He took with Him Peter and the two sons of Zebedee, and began to be grieved and distressed. Then He said to them, 'My soul is deeply grieved, to the point of death; remain here and keep watch with Me.' And He went a little beyond them and fell on His face and prayed, saying, 'My Father, if it is possible, let this cup pass from Me; yet not as I will, but as You will.' And He came to the disciples and found them sleeping, and said to Peter, 'So, you men could not keep watch with Me for one hour?'" **~ Matthew 26:36-40 NASB**

No spiritual leader is without the need for a firmly established and constant covering of intercession. Leaders absolutely cannot function to their fullest potential without the existence of strong prayer support. No matter what season of life or assignment ministers are called to; the *enthusiastic effort* of raising up prayer warriors must be of chief importance to the spiritual leader.

"Enthusiasm is one of the most powerful engines of success. When you do a thing, do it with all your might. Put your whole soul into it. Stamp it with your own personality. Be active, be energetic and faithful and you will accomplish your object. Nothing great was ever achieved without enthusiasm."
~ Ralph Waldo Emerson

You must begin now to assemble the saints to stand in your corner and pray for you as you contend for the souls of men. As the spiritual head of your ministry you need to have a sense of urgency to raise up a team responsible for covering you, your family and your ministry in prayer. The people of God need you to empower them to pray for YOU like never before. It is their high honor and noble assignment to so; and nobody else but you can impart the awareness of your desperation for their prayers.

It is time to quit relying on just a few sporadic seasons of prayer to get the job done. Many people who feel the call to pray are uninformed, unengaged and unaware of the enormous vision and scope of what God has called you to. It is time to mentor passionate men and women who will intercede for the ministry and mission to which you are called. You can and will overcome the coming rigors in the last-day as you are shielded with the blood of the lamb and the prayers of the saints.

As you begin to build the foundation of your prayer team you will need to select the right people. Note that from the beginning you don't have to have a lot of people in your inner prayer circle. Simply having two or three trustworthy and loyal prayer partners is better than having a room full of people who are more interested in their title, refuse to get on the same page, and really don't have your best interests at heart to begin with. I suggest starting with your closest friends and relatives. My wife, mother and mother in-law are among my top intercessors. Each one of them has enlisted reliable groups of seasoned and serious prayer warriors to pray over every event I request to be prayed for. They are available at a moment's notice (usually by text) and each of them diligently intercedes for every part of my ministry and family on the spot. Simultaneously, their circles of prayer are faithfully and continually active especially when called upon as well.

Be encouraged pastor and leader! God's best is just ahead but it will take an audacious band of militant prayer warriors to help advance you to the next level where the greatest victories you could ever imagine await you.

7 Crazy 'Charismaniac' Characters

At this juncture I feel it is important to briefly address the Pastor's altar/prayer team ministry. For training purposes it is good to have a solid reference to address the needs and qualifications of the prayer team (as we have covered so far and will continue to address in subsequent chapters). In the choosing of effective prayer teams (both for private sessions and public altar ministry), there are some *red flags* we should be prepared to identify in order to help head off the possible harmful outcomes that often result in this sensitive area of ministry.

Often, when the Holy Spirit is free to operate in a corporate meeting, people receive miraculous anointing, remarkable boldness, overflowing joy and irresistible enthusiasm. Yet, because we are all bent toward sin and selfishness, many people who experience the Holy Spirit's raw power sometimes also act weird. Their flesh gets in the way, and therefore misuse the gifts of the Spirit. I've seen this happen often during prayer/ministry times at a church altar. Because of poor training and a lack of mature leadership, things can get really out of hand when people come to the front of the auditorium for ministry. If this flakiness isn't immediately corrected, visitors will stop coming and your church will get a bad reputation. So, in a humorous light, here are seven people you should never allow to be in a ministry position in your church:[47]

1. Bulldozer Bertha – If this woman decides to pray for you at the altar, put one foot in front of the other, hold onto a chair and brace yourself. She intends to push you to the floor, one way or another. She's been told over and over that it is rude—not to mention dangerous—to push people during prayer. But she claims "the Spirit" turns her into a samurai warrior when the anointing comes on her. Steer clear.

Bulldozer Bertha is an accident waiting to happen.[47]

2. Shonda Wanda – I appreciate the gift of speaking in tongues, and there is a time and place for this gift in a church meeting. But it is not appropriate for a person to scream in tongues while they are ministering to someone at the altar. Shonda Wanda is notorious for offending visitors by pummeling them with noisy glossolalia. She should be reminded that seekers who come for prayer should be treated with sensitivity and respect—and that tongues is best reserved for private prayer times (see 1 Corinthians 14:18-19).[47]

3. Lascivious Larry – It is totally acceptable for people on a prayer team to lay hands on those who are seeking healing or comfort. But in this age of sexual perversion, some people are looking for a cheap thrill, even in church. Prayer ministers should be carefully trained on what kind of touch is appropriate during ministry times. We must have a zero tolerance policy for those who grope in the name of Jesus.[47]

4. Freak-Out Frances – It's a fact: Some people just act plain weird when they feel the anointing of the Holy Spirit. Some shake, others vibrate, others shriek or make birthing noises. I don't believe we should allow prayer ministers to carry on like this at the altar. The people who are entrusted with the job of praying for others should minister with gentleness and self-control. You will scare and confuse people if you are flailing your arms, jerking your torso or acting as if you have a nervous tic while you pray for them. This kind of immature behavior quenches the Holy Spirit (1 Thessalonians 5:19).[47]

5. Shrill Bill – The gift of prophecy can be a wonderful blessing—or it can be a total turn-off when the person prophesying is out of order. Nothing kills a church service like a prophet who sounds like he is channeling a banshee. Those who desire to minister in the gift of prophecy should learn to speak in a normal tone of voice—and they should convey love and Grace even when they are passionate. Don't allow angry or bitter prophets to ruin church for everyone else.[47]

6. Slick Rick – I believe it is scriptural to anoint people with oil when praying for healing (see James 5:14). But "anoint" does not mean dousing a person with two quarts of scented olive oil. I've seen some prayer ministers get so carried away with the oil that the poor people they were praying for left the church slimier than a pasta salad. A dab of anointing oil is enough![47]

7. Groovy Greta – God has gifted certain people in the arts—whether it is singing, songwriting, music or dance. But not all artistic expression belongs in church, and not everyone who thinks they are gifted should be given a platform. We've all been in situations where someone performed an awkward "praise dance" that should have been screened before it ended up on the church's live webcast. Don't allow the holy worship of God to be tainted by people who are selfishly seeking attention.[47]

The church is entering a new season in which God is raising the bar and calling us to a higher level of maturity. We must put away "childish things" (1 Cor. 13:11) and embrace not only the Holy Spirit's gifts but His fruit as well. We must ask the Holy Spirit to help us use wisdom and discernment regarding the flaky, the goofy and the just plain weird. Let's choose to operate in authentic spirituality that honors God and respects the people we are called to reach for Christ.

Pastors and Leaders should have their finger on the pulse of their prayer teams more than anyone else in order to foster unity and provide adequate and detailed information for those praying from outside the church (within the region or from long distance). This is not to say that pastors should be present at every prayer gathering. However, they should strive to initiate, develop systems of mentoring, oversee administration, and actually attend as many prayer gatherings as their schedule will allow. One rule of thumb is for pastors to prioritize their personal prayer team meetings in their itineraries. This way, they will not allow less important events to keep them from the precedence of leading this most vital ministry.[47]

Chapter 10

EFFECTIVE SPIRITUAL WARFARE

"Satan builds his strongholds in the shadows of our strengths." ~ **John Eldridge**

The vast subject of spiritual warfare deserves careful credence especially as it pertains to praying for our leaders. God called leaders possess supernatural giftings, talents and many other exceptional creative abilities, which place them at the top of the pack. However, the truth is the head of a spear faces the most wind resistance. In other words, along with these obvious strengths come various weaknesses and complex vulnerabilities. This is critical to understand in regards to those who stand at the front line of ministry. According to the dictionary, one of the meanings of the word *front-line* is *the most advanced, exposed, or conspicuous element in any activity or situation.* Satan assaults our front line leaders regularly. Therefore, we must be prepared to stand in the gap and wage valiant spiritual warfare for those who contend for the faith on our behalf.

Staying Faith Focused

It is my strong conviction that far too often spiritual warfare (particularly as it pertains to praying for our leaders) is presented from a tone of fear and foreboding. Many well meaning and sincere advocates of spiritual warfare often promote that unless we are successful in carrying it out in precisely prescribed formulas, our inadequate execution has the potential to be favorable for our enemy and fatal for us. This is the often-misunderstood ideology of spiritual warfare. To be certain, spiritual warfare is very real and there is a war to be waged. However, we often make it to be much more than it is and even something it isn't at all. When we have a correct New Testament understanding of spiritual warfare as it pertains to our New Covenant in Christ, we won't pray merely emotionally charged or formulaic prayers. Rather we will pray from a position of Spirit empowered authority, a deep settled confidence and an impenetrable fortress of peace! After all, the scriptures are clear that the battle isn't ours. The battle is the Lord's.

"The LORD does not deliver by sword or by spear; for the battle is the LORD'S..." ~ **1 Samuel 17:47 NASB**

"Thus says the LORD to you, 'Do not fear or be dismayed... For the battle is not yours but God's... You need not fight in

this battle; station yourselves, stand and see the salvation of the LORD on your behalf... Do not fear or be dismayed... For the LORD is with you." ~ **2 Chronicles 20:15-17 NASB**

Praying From the Victory

Essential to effective spiritual warfare is to understand this most basic fundamental truth: We don't pray for the victory; we pray FROM the victory. We are undefeatable champions in God's Grace and power seated in authority with Christ (Ephesians 2:6). To this, God has given us weapons to ENFORCE the victory that is already won.

"For the weapons of our warfare are not of the flesh, but divinely powerful for the destruction of fortresses. We are destroying speculations and every lofty thing raised up against the knowledge of God, and we are taking every thought captive to the obedience of Christ."
~ **2 Corinthians 10:3-5 NASB**

Our thoughts and perceptions are where the battle rages. Simply put, the mind is the battlefield. The scripture above tells us that we are destroying SPECULATIONS that have been raised against the knowledge of God. The devil speculates. That's all he can do. To this, we must simply deny his allegations and refutations by believing what God's Word says. The devil can only succeed in his efforts if he can get us to accept his claims of inevitability. The devil cannot commit any action without our consent. We give the devil permission to rule over our personal lives, our families and our churches when we believe his lies. This causes us to act anxiously, impulsively, reactively and hurtfully against others and ourselves.

Submit and Resist

When it comes to spiritual warfare the Bible is clear; we must *first* submit to God and secondly we must resist the devil, then He will flee from us.

"Submit therefore to God. Resist the devil and he will flee from you." ~ **James 4:7 NASB**

1. SUBMIT — According to the verse above, the **first** important factor in spiritual warfare is to submit to God. All too often we jump right into the resistance part before we settle the submission part. Many times the problem with unanswered prayers may not necessarily be with resisting the devil as much as it is submitting to God. When we walk in direct disobedience and defiance to God, our prayers will be hindered (I deal with this more on page 147). Therefore, if God has spoken or given you clear directives then obey Him and step out in faith. Your part is to simply obey God and leave all the consequences of your obedience in His hands.

Another factor of submitting to God is to simply accept what He says and act on it. When God's word says something about you, your family, your finances, or your future, speak that Word until it becomes *real* inside of you. Faith comes by hearing God's word.

"So then faith comes by hearing, and hearing by the word of God." ~ **Romans 10:17 NKJV**

I suggest reading the Bible out loud. As we speak and hear God's Word it takes root in us and as a result faith arises in our hearts that can move mountains. After all, when God says something, it's a done deal! We should simply accept what God says and resist what satan says.

2. RESIST — The **second** important factor regarding spiritual warfare is to resist the devil. The Greek word for *resist* is *anthistemi,* which is where we get our English word *antihistamine.* Our spiritual antihistamine is the Word of God. When we have the promises of God's Word deep in our spirit we can effectively resist the enemies lies. The Bible tells us that our warfare is all about resistance and standing firm on what God says.

"Therefore, take up the full armor of God, so that you will be able to RESIST in the evil day, and having done everything, to STAND FIRM." ~ **Ephesians 6:13 NASB**

Don't Fight the Devil

We must NEVER fight the devil when we pray. This wastes much needed spiritual energy. We must simply resist him and stand firm. Did you know we actually become stronger AS we resist? We burn out from trying to fight the devil but gain fresh momentum when we resist him. This is how we prevent weariness in spiritual warfare.

145

"And let us not be weary in well doing: for in due season we shall reap, if we faint not." ~ **Galatians 6:9 KJV**

Anxiety breeds weariness. Thus, when satan attempts to pick a fight, we must refuse his challenge. We need not bother to enter needless skirmishes or even speak to a defeated enemy. By avoiding a fight with the devil we allow God to handle our dirty work for us!

"But the LORD is with me like a mighty warrior; so my persecutors will stumble and not prevail. They will fail and be thoroughly disgraced; their dishonor will never be forgotten." ~ **Jeremiah 20:11 NIV**

"The LORD will march out like a mighty man, like a warrior he will stir up his zeal; with a shout he will raise the battle cry and will triumph over his enemies." ~ **Isaiah 42:13 NIV**

When we pray we must declare God's Word boldly. Our faith in God's Word is where we actualize our victories.

"For whatever is born of God overcomes the world and this is the victory that has overcome the world: OUR FAITH." ~ **1 John 5:4 NASB**

Our prayers always succeed when we stand on God's Word. Why? It is because God's word NEVER fails.

"So shall My word be that goes forth from My mouth; It shall not return to Me void, But it shall accomplish what I please, and it shall prosper in the thing for which I sent it."

Once we have the faith issue worked out, everything else falls into place. The devil is a liar and will attempt to argue with God's Word but He has no power to do so. Christ stripped him of His power, publicly humiliating him.

"Having disarmed principalities and powers, He made a public spectacle of them, triumphing over them in it."
~ **Colossians 2:15 NKJV**

Satan is merely an old, toothless lion lumbering around, roaring as loud as he can attempting to instill fear. By this he seeks opportunity to induce terror in us so we will lie down willfully thereby allowing him to devour us.

"The roaring of the lion and the voice of the fierce lion, and the teeth of the young lions are broken." ~ **Job 4:10 NASB**

"Be of sober spirit, be on the alert. Your adversary, the devil, prowls around LIKE A ROARING LION, seeking someone to devour. But RESIST him, FIRM IN YOUR FAITH..." ~ **1 Peter 5:7-8 NASB**

There's that word *resist* again. The way we resist satan's lies and enforce God's enactments is to submit to His Word with our thoughts, feelings and actions. The enemy cannot refute God's Word and therefore must give-in to its demands. Satan cannot defend us nor resist total defeat when we believe we already have what we pray for.

"This is the confidence which we have before Him, that, if we

ask anything according to His will, He hears us. And if we know that He hears us in whatever we ask, we know that we have the requests which we have asked from Him."
~ John 5:14-15 NASB

Fight the Good Fight

Fight the good fight of faith..."~ **1 Timothy 6:12 NASB**

God's Word says that our fight is a GOOD FIGHT. A bad fight is when the chips are down and the score is against us. Flailing our fists around and screaming into the heavens doesn't constitute a spiritual fight (although sometimes we do this in prayer). Our fight is to stand strong in faith believing in God's Word on the matter.

Can you imagine a frontline of soldiers just standing as they are being charged? This reminds me of the scene in the movie *Braveheart* when William Wallace (played by Mel Gibson) is screaming to his rag tag army of men to *"HOLD... HOLD... HOLD!"* And just about the moment the British forces are about to trample down the Scottish farmers, Wallace gives THE WORD and the men lift up their 30-foot spears as the Britt's plunge furlong into their horrible death.

This is what standing in faith is all about. It's holding fast to God's word no matter what our circumstances are. The devil is no match for the spoken Word of God from the mouth of a faith filled believer. He collides into God's Word like a Ferrari racing top speed and smashing into a brick wall. Too many a prayer meeting is nothing more than a fiasco of head banging and anxious fettering. However, when we pray with a SETTLED ASSURANCE that God is on our side; no mountain can stand before us and no man can stand against us. Hallelujah!

"Had it not been the LORD who was on our side when men rose up against us; then they would have swallowed us alive, when their anger was kindled against us."
~ Psalms 124:2-3 NASB

"What then shall we say to these things? If God is for us, who can be against us?" **~ Romans 8:31 NKJV**

"No weapon that is formed against you will prosper; and every tongue that accuses you in judgment you will condemn. This is the heritage of the servants of the LORD, and their vindication is from Me," declares the LORD." **~**
Isaiah 54:17 NASB

NO WEAPON formed against us can succeed. We are invincible. We can simply stand resolute, fully assured that we aren't going anywhere or giving up any ground. The fight has been fixed and we know WE WIN!

"The devil, who deceived them, was cast into the lake of fire and brimstone where the beast and the false prophet are. And they will be tormented day and night forever and ever." **~**
Isaiah 54:17 NASB

One Important Note... In spiritual warfare, we should never give a knee-jerk reaction to fear, doubt and unbelief. Rather we should respond in faith. Faith must be the motivating factor. Whenever our leaders face periodic setbacks, difficulties, drama, trauma and even a major crisis, we should approach spiritual warfare from a standpoint of calm assurance, boldness and victory. There is no need and frankly no real results in prayer when we frantically react. Rather we should firmly respond and take action! In this way, when we wage faith-filled spiritual warfare on behalf of our leaders based on faith in God's Word, our leaders in turn will experience powerful breakthroughs.

That's spiritual warfare in a *bombshell*.

Chapter 11

PRAYING GOD'S PROMISES FOR OUR LEADERS

"He has granted to us His precious and magnificent promises, so that by them you may become partakers of the divine nature." ~ **2 Peter 1:4 NASB**

Praying the scriptures, particularly the direct references to God's promises, is one of the most effective ways to cover our leaders. I have learned this both by praying for my leaders and also by being a direct recipient of those who prayed for me. God's Word is immutable and infallible. Therefore, we can stand strong on the foundation of all of God's promises.

"For all the promises of God in Him are Yes, and in Him Amen, to the glory of God through us."
~ **2 Corinthians 1:20-22 NKJV**

The scriptures are implicitly clear that we do not know what to pray (Romans 8:28). Therefore, we must be led by the Holy Spirit and the Word of the Living God as we intercede for our leaders. One main reason to use the Word of God when we pray is because the scriptures were inspired by the Holy Spirit. Every dotting of the 'i' and crossing of the 't' was penned as men were deeply moved by the Spirit.

"All Scripture is given by inspiration of God, and is profitable for doctrine, for reproof, for correction, for instruction in righteousness." ~ **2 Timothy 3:16 NKJV**

"For no prophecy was ever made by an act of human will, but men moved by the Holy Spirit spoke from God."
~ **2 Peter 1:21 NASB**

Praying the Scriptures Over Our Leaders

When we speak the scriptures over our leaders we literally declare over them what the Spirit Himself says and believes about them. The Bible is not merely words on paper but alive and active and relevant for our leaders RIGHT NOW! God's Word holds everything together including the spheres of influence that our leaders have jurisdiction over (Hebrews 11:13). Our leaders have not only been assigned to lead over physical realms but spiritual agencies. Their fight is not of this world and through our prayers we empower them to reign over principalities and powers that govern demonic thrones in wicked domains (Ephesians 6:12).

When God speaks, it is a sure thing. He never lies (Hebrews 6:18). The truth we have received through revelation, spoken over our leaders brings hidden things to light and sets them free (John 8:32). God uses scripture to reveal to us the hidden things that our leaders are dealing with and by that revelation we can cancel demonic assignments sent to them.

It is He who reveals the profound and hidden things; He knows what is in the darkness, and the light dwells with Him."
~ Daniel 2:22 NASB

Also, when the Word of God is spoken in prayer, it has a profound way of cutting to the core, slicing right to the specific issues surrounding our leaders.

"For the word of God is living and powerful, and sharper than any two-edged sword, piercing even to the division of soul and spirit, and of joints and marrow, and is a discerner of the thoughts and intents of the heart." **~ Hebrews 4:12 NKJV**

There is no doubting God's Word. There is something uncanny that happens when you have the written scriptures in your hand and read them aloud as you pray. The anointing that comes upon you is undeniable and will instill a deep confidence in you that God's promises are coming to pass for your leaders.

Pray The Promise of God's Presence

Great leaders of the Bible had one single characteristic that set them apart from every other leader. It was the key to their influence, prosperity, success and notable victories... God was with them.

"And the LORD was with Joseph, and he was a prosperous man; and he was in the house of his master the Egyptian. And his master saw that the LORD was with him, and that the LORD made all that he did to prosper in his hand."
~ Genesis 39:2-3 KJV

"The LORD was with Samuel as he grew up, and he let none of his words fall to the ground." ~ **1 Samuel 3:19 NIV**

And the LORD was with him (Hezekiah); wherever he went he prospered." ~ **2 Kings 18:7 NASB**

There are many more examples like these all throughout the Bible. Likewise for our leaders, the one single promise above all others that they need to be assured of is that God is with them. If they have to earn God's presence by their merits, what hope is there for them (or any of us for that matter)? God's abiding presence empowers leaders to obey Him and to lead effectively and efficiently. Leaders become fearful and less prone to take appropriate risks when they feel as if God's presence is not with them (Exodus 33:15). But the promise of scriptures clearly assures leaders that they have NO REASON to fear. God has not abandoned them and promises to remain and give them divine aid in all their leadership affairs.

"Do not fear, for I am with you; do not anxiously look about you, for I am your God. I will strengthen you, surely I will help you, surely I will uphold you with My righteous right hand.

154

"Behold, all those who are angered at you will be shamed and dishonored; those who contend with you will be as nothing and will perish. You will seek those who quarrel with you, but will not find them, those who war with you will be as nothing and non-existent. For I am the LORD your God, who upholds your right hand, Who says to you, 'Do not fear, I will help you.' " ~

Isaiah 41:10-13 NASB

Therefore, we should pray that God will assure our leaders, beyond any shadow of a doubt, of His commanding presence so they can perform to their optimal potential. When people sense that God's presence endorses leaders they are more settled, comforted and trusting while following them. We must also pray that God will continually soften the hearts of our leaders, as it is common for many to get hardened and bitter from the throes of ministry. We must ask God to help our leaders maintain a shepherd's heart. After all, God promised to give us shepherds that reflect His heart. He did not promise us great preachers, gifted singers, magnetic personalities or celebrity ministries. We need authentic people among us that exemplify God's standard of love and true leadership.

"Then I will give you shepherds after My own heart, who will feed you on knowledge and understanding."

~ Jeremiah 3:15 NASB

"I will also raise up shepherds over them and they will tend them; and they will not be afraid any longer, nor be terrified, nor will any be missing," declares the LORD."

~ Jeremiah 23:4 NASB

Promise and Provision Through Grace

To effectively pray God's promises for our leaders we must have a revelation of New Covenant Grace. The reason for this is while the promises of God are infallible our leaders are far from infallible. In fact they fail everyday. If we don't have a New Testament understanding of the gospel of Grace we will tend to pray judgmentally for our leaders and therefore pray the promises of God based upon conditions. Often we tend to judge our leaders before we pray for them. To this, we tend to withhold prayers based upon their performance. But the truth is, none of us deserve God's marvelous goodness. Likewise, it is not our leader's good behavior or performance that initiates the promises of God into their lives. It is the promises of God that initiates our leader's good behavior and performance. It's not what bad sinners we are; it's what a good Savior Jesus is! This is the fundamental premise of New Covenant Grace.

God's love and Grace are both unconditional and work in conjunction with one another. We must understand that God does not love our leaders because they are lovable. God loves them because HE is love and He blesses our leaders based upon His Grace and favor alone. While it is true that through wisdom and obedience, our leaders can experience more of the favor of God, they are still human creatures greatly in need of His Grace to empower them to walk the leader's walk. God's favor rests upon our leaders in order that they may receive the promises He has granted. Our leaders cannot lead well unless God's Grace provides them the power to do so. Our leader's good works do not secure God's love and favor for their ministry. God's love and favor empowers our leaders and frees them to perform mighty exploits. We must pray with this attitude. If a leader is failing, pray that God's strength will renew them. We must continue to pray the promises of God for our leaders in spite of their shortcomings. Why? Because when Gods fulfills his promises, it is His goodness that draws our leaders to a lifestyle of repentance.

"Or do you despise the riches of His goodness, forbearance, and longsuffering, not knowing that the goodness of God leads you to repentance?" ~ **Romans 2:4 NKJV**

In the Old Covenant, the promises of God were contingent upon obedience. In the New Covenant of Grace the ability to obey God is contingent upon receiving the promises FIRST! For religious mindsets Grace is difficult to believe, receive, retain and release. It's a challenge to wrap your minds around the abstract concept of Grace. That is why we must simply accept that God loves and forgives us. The promises of God are impossible to *achieve*. We must simply *receive* them. In order to enjoy all that God's promises have to offer, we must believe and receive them for ourselves and then pray them for our leaders regardless of their shortcomings. The essence of the Law is demand. The essence of Grace is supply. God's supplies His promises in order that the demands of the Law and life can be met. We must get this revelation or we will never fully pray and receive all that God has for our leaders.

The new covenant blood of Jesus procures our leaders to better serve people in humility, love and authority. We should not pray for our leaders based on their ability and faithfulness to serve and lead, but because they require God's promises in order to faithfully serve and lead.

I have written a powerful and compelling 328-page book entitled GRACE WORKS that offers deeper insight in much greater detail regarding the gospel of Grace. People everywhere are reading it and are being totally set free by the amazing revelation of Grace. You can order a copy by logging onto www.tonysutherland.com.

Chapter 12

SCRIPTURE PROMISES
FOR LEADERS

"To be able to lead others, a man must be willing to go forward alone." ~ **Harry Truman**

More times than we realize our leaders simply feel abandoned and alone. Telling your leader that you are praying the promises of God for their life can instantly refresh and revive them for the journey. As you intercede for your pastors and leaders, I highly suggest using the passages in this chapter, along with the weekly and monthly prayer schedule at the end of this book (Chapter 14 & 15) as a springboard for your prayers. In fact the weekly and monthly prayer schedules were inspired from the following scriptural promises. A note to leaders: It would do you well to read these passages aloud and even post a few of them in the places you most frequent (bathroom mirror, car dashboard, office, computer screen, etc.) Regularly confess aloud and remind yourself of what God says on the matter. These passages will powerfully encourage and strengthen you in your leadership on a daily basis. Some of the following scriptures are direct prophetic references to Israel and the Messiah. However, leaders (and all believers) have been made joint heirs of the inheritance that belongs to Jesus (Romans 8:17). Therefore, we too are recipients of all God's promises.

Scripture Promises

The following promises apply to all believers. However, these references can be directly applied to the exceptional and distinctive needs of ministry leaders. These passages can also be used as powerful scriptural confessions of faith for the minister. Boldly speak them aloud for every situation you face.

"Blessed be God Most High, Who has delivered your enemies into your hand." ~ **Genesis 14:20 NASB**

"I will multiply you exceedingly." ~ **Genesis 17:2 NASB**

"Indeed I will greatly bless you... and your seed shall possess the gate of their enemies." ~ **Genesis 22:17 NASB**

"I will send My terror ahead of you, and throw into confusion all the people among whom you come, and I will make all your enemies turn their backs to you." ~ **Genesis 23:27 NASB**

"So therefore, do not be afraid; I will provide for you and your little ones." ~ **Genesis 50:21 NASB**

"The LORD will fight for you, and you shall hold your peace."
~ Exodus 14:14 NASB

"Behold, I am going to send an angel before you to guard you along the way and to bring you into the place which I have prepared." **~ Exodus 23:20 NASB**

"But go now, lead the people where I told you. Behold, My angel shall go before you..." **~ Exodus 32:34 NASB**

"Then I will give you rain in due season, and the land shall yield her increase, and the trees of the field shall yield their fruit."
~ Leviticus 32:34 KJV

"May the LORD, the God of your fathers, increase you a thousand-fold more than you are and bless you, just as He has promised you!" **~ Deuteronomy 1:11 NASB**

"Then I will give you the rain for your land in its season, the early rain and the latter rain, that you may gather in your grain, your new wine, and your oil." **~ Deuteronomy 11:14 NASB**

"The LORD himself goes before you and will be with you; he will never leave you nor forsake you. Do not be afraid; do not be discouraged." **~ Deuteronomy 31:8 NIV**

"The LORD will open the heavens, the storehouse of his bounty, to send rain on your land in season and to bless all the work of your hands. You will lend to many nations but will borrow from none." **~ Deuteronomy 28:12 NIV**

"The LORD your God will make you most prosperous in all the work of your hands..." ~ **Deuteronomy 30:9 NIV**

"The eternal God is a dwelling place, and underneath are the everlasting arms; and He drove out the enemy from before you..." ~ **Deuteronomy 33:27 NASB**

"My God, my rock, in whom I take refuge, My shield and the horn of my salvation, my stronghold and my refuge; My savior, You save me from violence." ~ **2 Samuel 22:3 NASB**

"For the eyes of the LORD move to and fro throughout the earth that He may strongly support those whose heart is completely His." ~ **2 Chronicles 16:9 NASB**

"Thus says the LORD to you, 'Do not fear or be dismayed... For the battle is not yours but God's... You need not fight in this battle; station yourselves, stand and see the salvation of the LORD on your behalf... Do not fear or be dismayed... For the LORD is with you." ~ **2 Chronicles 20:15-17 NASB**

"The God of Heaven will give us success; therefore we His servants will arise and build." ~ **Nehemiah 2:20 NASB**

"Though your beginning was insignificant, yet your end will increase greatly." ~ **Job 8:7 NASB**

"Ask of Me, and I will give You the nations for Your inheritance, and the ends of the earth for Your possession." ~ **Psalms 2:8 NKJV**

"But You, O LORD, are a shield about me, my glory, and the One who lifts my head... All my enemies will be ashamed and greatly dismayed; they shall turn back, they will suddenly be ashamed." ~ **Psalms 3:3-7 NASB**

"For it is You who blesses the righteous man, O LORD, You surround him with favor as with a shield."
~ **Psalms 5:12 NASB**

"LORD, you alone are my inheritance, my cup of blessing. You guard all that is mine... I know the LORD is always with me. I will not be shaken, for he is right beside me."
~ **Psalms 16:5-8 NASB**

"The LORD is my rock and my fortress and my deliverer, My God, my rock, in whom I take refuge; my shield and the horn of my salvation, my stronghold." ~ **Psalms 18:2 NASB**

"He delivers me from my enemies; surely You lift me above those who rise up against me; You rescue me from the violent man." ~ **Psalms 18:48 NASB**

"May He send you help from the sanctuary and support you from Zion!" ~ **Psalms 20:2 NASB**

"The LORD is my light and my salvation; Whom shall I fear? The LORD is the defense of my life; Whom shall I dread? When evildoers came upon me to devour my flesh, My adversaries and my enemies, they stumbled and fell. Though a host encamp against me, My heart will not fear; Though war arise against me, In spite of this I shall be confident... For in

the day of trouble He will conceal me in His tabernacle; In the secret place of His tent He will hide me; He will lift me up on a rock. And now my head will be lifted up above my enemies around me, And I will offer in His tent sacrifices with shouts of joy; I will sing, yes, I will sing praises to the LORD."
~ Psalms 27:1-6 NASB

"O LORD, by Your favor You have made my mountain to stand strong." **~ Psalms 30:7 NASB**

"Let them shout for joy and rejoice, who favor my vindication; and let them say continually, 'The LORD be magnified, Who delights in the prosperity of His servant.' "
~ Psalms 35:27 NASB

"As for me, You uphold me in my integrity, and You set me in Your presence forever." **~ Psalms 41:12 NASB**

"But You have saved us from our adversaries, and You have put to shame those who hate us." **~ Psalms 44:7 NASB**

"Let the favor of the Lord our God be upon us; and confirm for us the work of our hands; Yes, confirm the work of our hands." **~ Psalms 90:17 NASB**

"You who sit down in the High God's presence, spend the night in Shaddai's shadow, say this: 'God, you're my refuge. I trust in you and I'm safe!' That's right—he rescues you from hidden traps, shields you from deadly hazards. His huge outstretched arms protect you—under them you're perfectly safe; his arms fend off all harm. Fear nothing—not wild wolves

in the night, not flying arrows in the day, not disease that prowls through the darkness, not disaster that erupts at high noon. Even though others succumb all around, drop like flies right and left, no harm will even graze you. You'll stand untouched, Watch it all from a distance, watch the wicked turn into corpses. Yes, because God's your refuge, the High God your very own home, evil can't get close to you, harm can't get through the door. He ordered his angels to guard you wherever you go. If you stumble, they'll catch you; their job is to keep you from falling. You'll walk unharmed among lions and snakes, and kick young lions and serpents from the path."
~ Psalms 91:1-15 THE MESSAGE

"For He has shattered gates of bronze and cut bars of iron asunder." **~ Psalms 107:15-16 NASB**

"May the LORD give you increase, you and your children."
~ Psalms 115:14 NASB

"The LORD keeps watch over you as you come and go, both now and forever." **~ Psalms 121:8 NLT**

"May peace be within your walls, and prosperity within your palaces." **~ Psalms 122:7 NASB**

"For the LORD will vindicate his people and have compassion on his servants." **~ Psalms 135:14 NIV**

"He makes peace in your borders; He satisfies you with the finest of the wheat." **~ Psalms 147:14 NASB**

"So you will find favor and good repute in the sight of God and man." ~ **Proverbs 3:4 NASB**

"Your body will glow with health, your very bones will vibrate with life. Honor God with everything you own; give him the first and the best. Your barns will burst, your wine vats will brim over." ~ **Proverbs 3:7-10 THE MESSAGE**

"Blessings are on the head of the righteous... The memory of the righteous is blessed... " ~ **Proverbs 10:6-7 NASB**

"In the light of a king's face is life, and his favor is like a cloud with the spring rain." ~ **Proverbs 16:5 NASB**

"When you pass through the waters, I will be with you; And through the rivers, they shall not overflow you. When you walk through the fire, you shall not be burned, Nor shall the flame scorch you." ~ **Isaiah 42:1 NKJV**

"I will go before you and make the rough places smooth; I will shatter the doors of bronze and cut through their iron bars."
~ **Isaiah 45:2 NASB**

"He energizes those who get tired, gives fresh strength to dropouts. For even young people tire and drop out, young folk in their prime stumble and fall. But those who wait upon God get fresh strength. They spread their wings and soar like eagles, they run and don't get tired, they walk and don't lag behind." ~ **Isaiah 49:29-31 THE MESSAGE**

"For the LORD will go ahead of you; yes, the God of Israel will protect you from behind. See, my servant will prosper; he will be highly exalted." ~ **Isaiah 52:12-13 NLT**

"Fear not, for you will not be put to shame; and do not feel humiliated, for you will not be disgraced..."
~ **Isaiah 54:4 NASB**

"No weapon turned against you will succeed. You will silence every voice raised up to accuse you. These benefits are enjoyed by the servants of the LORD; their vindication will come from me. I, the LORD, have spoken!"
~ **Isaiah 54:17 NLT**

"Instead of your shame you will have a double portion, and instead of humiliation they will shout for joy over their portion. Therefore they will possess a double portion in their land, everlasting joy will be theirs." ~ **Isaiah 61:7 NASB**

"For he will be like a tree planted by the water, that extends its roots by a stream and will not fear when the heat comes; but its leaves will be green, And it will not be anxious in a year of drought Nor cease to yield fruit." ~ **Jeremiah 17:8 NASB**

"For I satisfy the weary ones and refresh everyone who languishes." ~ **Jeremiah 31:25 NASB**

"Behold, I will bring it health and cure, and I will cure them, and will reveal unto them the abundance of peace and truth."
~ **Jeremiah 33:6 KJV**

"I will remove all proud and arrogant people from among you. There will be no more haughtiness on my holy mountain."
~ Zephaniah 3:1 NLT

"I will give you a good name, a name of distinction, among all the nations of the earth, as I restore your fortunes before their very eyes. I, the LORD, have spoken!" **~ Zephaniah 3:20 NLT**

"These signs will accompany those who have believed: in My name they will cast out demons, they will speak with new tongues; they will pick up serpents, and if they drink any deadly poison, it will not hurt them; they will lay hands on the sick, and they will recover." **~ Mark 16:17-18 NASB**

"And I will do whatever you ask in my name, so that the Son may bring glory to the Father. You may ask me for anything in my name, and I will do it..." **~ John 14:13-14 NIV**

"Peace I leave with you; my peace I give you. I do not give to you as the world gives. Do not let your hearts be troubled and do not be afraid." **~ John 14:27 NIV**

"Ask, using my name, and you will receive, and you will have abundant joy." **~ John 16:24 NLT**

"So the church throughout all Judea and Galilee and Samaria enjoyed peace, being built up; and going on in the fear of the Lord and in the comfort of the Holy Spirit, it continued to increase." **~ Acts 9:31 NASB**

"Those who receive the abundance of Grace and of the gift of righteousness will reign in life through the One, Jesus Christ."
~ Romans 5:17 NASB

"How beautiful are the feet of those who bring good news of good things!" **~ Romans 10:15 NASB**

"Now may the God of hope fill you with all joy and peace in believing, so that you will abound in hope by the power of the Holy Spirit." **~ Romans 15:13 NASB**

"The God of peace will soon crush Satan under your feet. The Grace of our Lord Jesus be with you." **~ Romans 16:20 NASB**

"And God is able to make all Grace abound toward you, that you, always having all sufficiency in all things, may have an abundance for every good work." **~ 2 Corinthians 9:8 NASB**

"I was made a minister, according to the gift of God's Grace which was given to me according to the working of His power." **~ Ephesians 3:7 NASB**

"For I know that this will turn out for my deliverance through your prayers and the provision of the Spirit of Jesus Christ."
~ Philippians 1:19 NASB

"And my God shall supply all your need according to His riches in glory by Christ Jesus." **~ Philippians 4:19 NKJV**

"Faithful is He who calls you, and He also will bring it to pass."
~1 Thessalonians 5:24 NASB

"But the Lord is faithful, and He will strengthen and protect you from the evil one." ~ **2 Thessalonians 3:3 NASB**

"For He Himself has said, I will never leave you nor forsake you. So we may boldly say: 'The LORD is my helper; I will not fear. What can man do to me?' " ~ **Hebrews 13:5-6 NKJV**

"After you have suffered for a little while, the God of all Grace, who called you to His eternal glory in Christ, will Himself perfect, confirm, strengthen and establish you."
~ **1 Peter 5:10 NASB**

"But you have an anointing from the Holy One... As for you, the anointing, which you received from Him abides in you."
~ **1 John 2:20 NASB**

"Beloved, I pray that in all respects you may prosper and be in good health, just as your soul prospers." ~ **3 John 1:2 NASB**

Chapter 13

PRAYER SCRIPTURES

"And the Lord said unto me, 'Behold, I have put my words in thy mouth.' " ~ **Jeremiah 1:9 KJV**

One of the most effective ways to pray is to pray the scriptures. It takes faith to move mountains and faith only comes through the hearing of God's word (*Romans 10:17*). We must allow God to put His words in our mouths as we pray. It is one thing to pray with our words but it is entirely another thing to pray GOD'S WORDS. When we allow God's wisdom to direct our prayers, we have the assurance we need that our prayers will be answered. God's word is His will and when we know that we have prayed His will, we have complete assurance that our prayers will be answered.

"This is the confidence which we have before Him, that, if we ask anything according to His will, He hears us. And if we know

that He hears us in whatever we ask, we know that we have the requests, which we have asked from Him."
~1 John 5:14-15 NASB

Great inspiration and tenacity in prayer comes when God reveals a verse that burns in the heart of the intercessor. Praying God's word over leaders, churches, communities, cities and nations has brought tremendous victories throughout the history of the Church. Derek Prince in his book *Shaping History Through Prayer and Fasting* says:

> *"Christ is the King of kings and the Lord of lords. He is the ruler of Earth's rulers and the governor over Earth's governments. His authority over all earthly governments is made available in His name to the church - The assembly of His believing people. As Moses stretched forth his rod on God's behalf over Egypt, so the church by its prayers stretches forth Christ's authority over the nations and their rulers."*

Therefore in light of the critical importance of the scriptures in prayer, I have provided you with an arsenal of scriptures to motivate you as you pray. These passages are not prayers per-se. They are provided primarily to empower and give Biblical context and revelation to you as you pray in faith.

Old Testament Prayer Scriptures

"Then he said, "Let me go, for the dawn is breaking" But he said, "I will not let you go unless you bless me.""

~ **Genesis 32:26 NASB**

"Then Moses and Aaron went out from Pharaoh, and Moses cried to the LORD concerning the frogs which He had inflicted upon Pharaoh. The LORD did according to the word of Moses, and the frogs died out of the houses, the courts, and the fields" ~ **Exodus 8:12-13 NASB**

"The people therefore cried out to Moses, and Moses prayed to the LORD and the fire died out." ~ **Numbers 11:2 NASB**

"Then Joshua spoke to the LORD in the day when the LORD delivered up the Amorites before the sons of Israel, and he said in the sight of Israel, "O sun, stand still at Gibeon, And O moon in the valley of Aijalon." So the sun stood still, and the moon stopped, until the nation avenged themselves of their enemies... And the sun stopped in the middle of the sky and did not hasten to go down for about a whole day."
~ **Joshua 10:12-13 NASB**

"Then Samson called to the LORD and said, "O Lord GOD, please remember me and please strengthen me just this time, O God, that I may at once be avenged of the Philistines for my two eyes." Samson grasped the two middle pillars on which the house rested, and braced himself against them, the one with his right hand and the other with his left. And Samson said, "Let me die with the Philistines!" And he bent with all his might so that the house fell on the lords and all the people who were in it. So the dead whom he killed at his death were more than those whom he killed in his life." ~ **Judges 16: 28-30 NASB**

"She (Hannah), greatly distressed, prayed to the LORD and wept bitterly. She made a vow and said, "O LORD of hosts, if You will indeed look on the affliction of Your maidservant and remember me, and not forget Your maidservant, but will give Your maidservant a son, then I will give him to the LORD all the days of his life, and a razor shall never come on his head." Now it came about, as she continued praying before the LORD, that Eli was watching her mouth. As for Hannah, she was speaking in her heart, only her lips were moving, but her voice was not heard. So Eli thought she was drunk. Then Eli said to her, "How long will you make yourself drunk? Put away your wine from you." But Hannah replied, "No, my lord, I am a woman oppressed in spirit; I have drunk neither wine nor strong drink, but I have poured out my soul before the LORD. "Do not consider your maidservant as a worthless woman, for I have spoken until now out of my great concern and provocation." Then Eli answered and said, "Go in peace; and may the God of Israel grant your petition that you have asked of Him." She said, "Let your maidservant find favor in your sight." So the woman went her way and ate, and her face was no longer sad. Then they arose early in the morning and worshiped before the LORD, and returned again to their house in Ramah. And Elkanah had relations with Hannah his wife, and the LORD remembered her. It came about in due time, after Hannah had conceived, that she gave birth to a son; and she named him Samuel, saying, "Because I have asked him of the LORD."" ~1 Samuel 1:11-20 NASB

"In those days Hezekiah became mortally ill. And Isaiah the prophet the son of Amoz came to him and said to him, "Thus says the LORD, 'Set your house in order, for you shall die and not live.'" Then he turned his face to the wall and prayed to the LORD, saying, "Remember now, O LORD, I beseech You, how I have walked before You in truth and with a whole heart and have done what is good in Your sight." And Hezekiah wept bitterly. Before Isaiah had gone out of the middle court, the word of the LORD came to him, saying, "Return and say to Hezekiah the leader of My people, Thus says the LORD, the God of your father David, 'I have heard your prayer, I have seen your tears; behold, I will heal you. On the third day you shall go up to the house of the LORD. I will add fifteen years to your life, and I will deliver you and this city from the hand of the king of Assyria; and I will defend this city for My own sake and for My servant David's sake.'" ~ **2 Kings 20:1-6 NASB**

"Ask of Me, and I will surely give the nations as Your inheritance, and the very ends of the earth as Your possession." ~ **Psalms 2:8 NASB**

"I love the LORD, because He hears my voice and my supplications. Because He has inclined His ear to me, therefore I shall call upon Him as long as I live."
~ **Psalms 116:1-2 NASB**

"I searched for a man among them who would build up the wall and stand in the gap before Me for the land, so that I would not destroy it; but I found no one."
~ **Ezekiel 22:30 NASB**

"And I will cause him to draw near, and he shall approach unto me: for who is this that engaged his heart to approach unto me?" saith the LORD." ~ **Jeremiah 30:21 KJV**

"So I gave my attention to the Lord God to seek Him by prayer and supplications, with fasting, sackcloth and ashes… Then He said to me, "Do not be afraid, Daniel, for from the first day that you set your heart on understanding this and on humbling yourself before your God, your words were heard, and I have come in response to your words."" ~ **Daniel 9:3-10:12 NASB**

"Thus says the LORD, the Holy One of Israel, and his Maker: "Ask Me about the things to come concerning My sons, and you shall commit to Me the work of My hands.""
~ **Isaiah 45:11 NASB**

"You will seek Me and find Me when you search for Me with all your heart." ~ **Jeremiah 29:13 NASB**

"Call to Me and I will answer you, and I will tell you great and mighty things, which you do not know."
~ ***Jeremiah 33:3 NASB***

"I called out of my distress to the LORD, and He answered me I cried for help from the depth of Sheol; You heard my voice. For You had cast me into the deep, into the heart of the seas, and the current engulfed me, all Your breakers and billows passed over me. So I said, 'I have been expelled from Your sight Nevertheless I will look again toward Your holy temple." Water encompassed me to the point of death, the great deep engulfed me, weeds were wrapped around my head. I*

descended to the roots of the mountains the earth with its bars was around me forever, but You have brought up my life from the pit, O LORD my God. While I was fainting away, I remembered the LORD, and my prayer came to You, Into Your holy temple." ~ **Jonah 2:2-7 NASB**

"But as for me, I will watch expectantly for the LORD; I will wait for the God of my salvation. My God will hear me."
~ **Micah 7:7 NASB**

New Testament Prayer Scriptures

"Ask, and it will be given to you; seek, and you will find; knock, and it will be opened to you. For everyone who asks receives, and he who seeks finds, and to him who knocks it will be opened… If you then, being evil, know how to give good gifts to your children, how much more will your Father who is in heaven give what is good to those who ask Him."
~ **Matthew 7:7-11 NASB**

"But you, when you pray, go into your inner room, close your door and pray to your Father who is in secret, and your Father who sees what is done in secret will reward you. And when you are praying, do not use meaningless repetition as the Gentiles do, for they suppose that they will be heard for their many words. So do not be like them; for your Father knows what you need before you ask Him. Pray, then, in this way: Our Father who is in heaven, Hallowed be Your name. Your kingdom come, Your will be done, on earth as it is in Heaven. Give us this day our daily bread and forgive us our debts, as

we also have forgiven our debtors. And do not lead us into temptation, but deliver us from evil. For Yours is the kingdom and the power and the glory forever. Amen. For if you forgive others for their transgressions, your heavenly Father will also forgive you. But if you do not forgive others, then your Father will not forgive your transgressions. Whenever you fast, do not put on a gloomy face as the hypocrites do for they neglect their appearance so that they will be noticed by men when they are fasting. Truly I say to you, they have their reward in full. But you, when you fast, anoint your head and wash your face so that your fasting will not be noticed by men, but by your Father who is in secret; and your Father who sees what is done in secret will reward you." ~ **Matthew 6:6-18 NASB**

"Therefore, pray the Lord of the harvest to send out laborers into His harvest." ~ **Matthew 9:38 NKJV**

"Truly I say to you, whatever you bind on earth shall have been bound in heaven; and whatever you loose on earth shall have been loosed in heaven. Again I say to you, that if two of you agree on earth about anything that they may ask, it shall be done for them by My Father who is in Heaven. For where two or three have gathered together in My name, I am there in their midst." ~ **Matthew 18:18-20 NASB**

"And all things you ask in prayer, believing, you will receive."
~ **Matthew 21:22 NASB**

Jesus answered saying to them, "Have faith in God. Truly I say to you, whoever says to this mountain, 'Be taken up and cast into the sea,' and does not doubt in his heart, but believes that what he says is going to happen, it will be granted him. Therefore I say to you, all things for which you pray and ask, believe that you have received them, and they will be granted you. Whenever you stand praying, forgive, if you have anything against anyone, so that your Father who is in Heaven will also forgive you your transgressions. But if you do not forgive, neither will your Father who is in heaven forgive your transgressions." ~ **Mark 11:22-26 NASB**

"Now He was telling them a parable to show that at all times they ought to pray and not to lose heart, saying, 'In a certain city there was a judge who did not fear God and did not respect man. There was a widow in that city and she kept coming to him, saying, 'Give me legal protection from my opponent.' For a while he was unwilling; but afterward he said to himself, 'Even though I do not fear God nor respect man, yet because this widow bothers me, I will give her legal protection, otherwise by continually coming she will wear me out.' And the Lord said, 'Hear what the unrighteous judge said. Now, will not God bring about justice for His elect who cry to Him day and night, and will He delay long over them. I tell you that He will bring about justice for them quickly. However, when the Son of Man comes, will He find faith on the earth?"
~Luke 18:1-8 NASB

"Whatever you ask in My name, that will I do, so that the Father may be glorified in the Son. If you ask Me anything in My name, I will do it." ~**John 14:13-14 NASB**

"If you abide in Me, and My words abide in you, ask whatever you wish, and it will be done for you." ~ **John 15:7 NASB**

"Truly, truly, I say to you, if you ask the Father for anything in My name, He will give it to you." ~ **John 16:24 NASB**

"These all with one mind were continually devoting themselves to prayer..." ~ **Acts 1:14 NASB**

"So Peter was kept in the prison, but prayer for him was being made fervently by the church to God... "Now I know for sure that the Lord has sent forth His angel and rescued me from the hand of Herod and from all that the Jewish people were expecting." And when he realized this he went to the house of Mary, the mother of John who was also called Mark, where many were gathered together and were praying... and when they had opened the door they saw him and were amazed. But motioning to them with his hand to be silent, he described to them how the Lord had led him out of the prison..."
~ Acts 12:5-17 NASB

"In the same way the Spirit also helps our weakness; for we do not know how to pray as we should, but the Spirit Himself intercedes for us with groanings too deep for words. And He who searches the hearts knows what the mind of the Spirit is because He intercedes for the saints according to the will of God. And we know that God causes all things to work together for good to those who love God, to those who are called according to His purpose." ~ **Romans 8:26-18 NASB**

"Therefore I urge you, brethren, by the mercies of God, to present your bodies a living and holy sacrifice, acceptable to God, which is your spiritual service of worship… rejoicing in hope, persevering in tribulation, devoted to prayer."
~ **Romans 12:1,12 NASB**

"Now I urge you, brethren, by our Lord Jesus Christ and by the love of the Spirit, to strive together with me in your prayers to God for me, that I may be rescued from those who are disobedient… and that my service… may prove acceptable to the saints; so that I may come to you in joy by the will of God and find refreshing rest in your company."
~**Romans 15:30-32 NASB**

"You also joining in helping us through your prayers, so that thanks may be given by many persons on our behalf for the favor bestowed on us through the prayers of many."
~ **2 Corinthians 1:11 NASB**

"Now to Him who is able to do far more abundantly beyond all that we ask or think, according to the power that works within us." ~ **Ephesians 3:20 NASB**

"With all prayer and petition pray at all times in the Spirit, and with this in view, be on the alert with all perseverance and petition for all the saints, and pray on my behalf, that utterance may be given to me in the opening of my mouth, to make known with boldness the mystery of the gospel, for which I am an ambassador in chains; that in proclaiming it I may speak boldly, as I ought to speak." ~ **Ephesians 6:18-20 NASB**

"Be anxious for nothing, but in everything by prayer and supplication with thanksgiving let your requests be made known to God. And the peace of God, which surpasses all comprehension, will guard you hearts and your minds in Christ Jesus." ~ **Philippians 4:6-7 NASB**

"Devote yourselves to prayer, keeping alert in it with an attitude of thanksgiving; praying at the same time for us as well, that God will open up to us a door for the word, so that we may speak forth the mystery of Christ, for which I have also been imprisoned; that I may make it clear in the way I ought to speak... Epaphras, who is one of your number, a bondslave of Jesus Christ, sends you his greetings, always laboring earnestly for you in his prayers, that you may stand perfect and fully assured in all the will of God."
~ **Colossians 4:2-4,12 NASB**

"We night and day keep praying most earnestly... So that He may establish your hearts without blame in holiness..."
~**1 Thessalonians 3:10-13 NASB**

"Pray without ceasing." ~ **1 Thessalonians 5:17 NASB**

"Finally, brethren, pray for us that the word of the Lord will spread rapidly and be glorified, just as it did also with you; and that we will be rescued from perverse and evil men; for not all have faith." ~ **2 Thessalonians 3:1-3 NASB**

"First of all, then, I urge that entreaties and prayers, petitions and thanksgivings, be made on behalf of all men... For this I was appointed a preacher and an apostle... as a teacher of the

Gentiles in faith and truth. Therefore I want the men in every place to pray, lifting up holy hands, without wrath and dissension." ~ **1 Timothy 2:1-8 NASB**

"In the days of His flesh, He offered up both prayers and supplications with loud crying and tears to the One able to save Him from death, and He was heard because of His piety... And having been made perfect, He became to all those who obey Him the source of eternal salvation."
~Hebrews 5:7 NASB

"But without faith it is impossible to please Him, for he who comes to God must believe that He is, and that He is a rewarder of those who diligently seek Him."
~ Hebrews 11:6 NKJV

"If any of you lacks wisdom, let him ask of God, who gives to all generously and without reproach, and it will be given to him. But he must ask in faith without any doubting, for the one who doubts is like the surf of the sea, driven and tossed by the wind. For that man ought not to expect that he will receive anything from the Lord" ~ **James 1:5-7 NASB**

"You do not have because you do not ask. You ask and do not receive, because you ask with wrong motives, so that you may spend it on your pleasures." ~ **James 4:2-3 NASB**

"And the prayer offered in faith will make the sick person well; the Lord will raise them up. If they have sinned, they will be forgiven... The prayer of a righteous person is powerful and effective. Elijah was a human being, even as we are. He prayed

earnestly that it would not rain, and it did not rain on the land for three and a half years. Again he prayed, and the heavens gave rain, and the earth produced its crops."
~ James 5:15-18 NIV

"For the eyes of the Lord are on the righteous and his ears are attentive to their prayer..." **~ 1 Peter 3:12 NIV**

"And whatever we ask we receive from Him, because we keep His commandments and do the things that are pleasing in His sight." **~ 1 John 3:22 NASB**

"This is the confidence which we have before Him, that, if we ask anything according to His will, He hears us. And if we know that He hears us in whatever we ask, we know that we have the requests which we have asked from Him."
~ 1 John 5:14-15 NASB

Chapter 14

PRAYER QUOTES

"Prayer does not fit us for the greater work. Prayer is the greater work." ~ **Oswald Chambers**

The following quotes are provided to inspire you to pray more fervently for your leaders. Each one of these profound statements has come from the experience of the people who spoke them. Their lives are their message. These men and women of God have proven that you cannot stumble while your on your knees. May these quotes spawn you to more profound thought and wisdom. Some quotes below have previously been used in this book.

"God shapes the world by prayer." ~ **E.M. Bounds**

"We truly pray only when our heart's desire is equal to our words." ~ **Cecil B. Knight**

"Prayer is not overcoming God's reluctance; it is laying hold of His willingness." ~ **T.F. Tenney**

"Prayerless men have never been used of God."
~ **E.M. Bounds**

"Apostasy generally begins at the prayer closet door."
~ **Philip Henry**

"All ability to talk to men is measured by the ability with which a preacher can talk to God for men. He who ploughs not in his closet, will never reap in his pulpit." ~ **E.M. Bounds**

"The low, feeble life of the church, the lack of openness to the power of the Holy Spirit for conversion and holiness, is all owing to the lack of prayer." ~ **Andrew Murray**

"The time of business does not with me differ from the time of prayer." ~ **Brother Lawrence**

"The greatest and the best talent that God gives to any man or woman in this world is the talent of prayer."
~ **Principal Alexander Whyte**

"It is only when the whole heart is gripped with the passion of prayer that the life-giving fire descends, for none but the earnest man gets access to the ear of God." ~ **E.M. Bounds**

"More and better praying will bring the surest and readiest triumph to God's cause; feeble, formal, listless praying brings decay and death. The church has its sheet-anchor in the closet; its magazine stores are there." ~ **John Foster**

"The potency of prayer hath subdued the strength of fire; it hath bridled the rage of lions hushed anarchy to rest, extinguished wars, appeased the elements, expelled demons, burst the chains of death, expanded the gates of Heaven, assuaged diseases, repelled frauds, rescued cities from destruction, stayed the sun in its course, and arrested the progress of the thunderbolt. Prayer is all-efficient panoply, a treasure undiminished, a mine, which is never exhausted, a sky unobscured by clouds, a heaven unruffled by the storm. It is the root, the fountain, the mother of a thousand blessings."
~ John Chrysostom

"The more I get to pray, the more God gets to do."
~ Esther Ilnisky

"The prayers of holy men appease God's wrath, drive away temptations, resist and overcome the devil, procure the ministry and service of angels, rescind the decrees of God. Prayer cures sickness and obtains pardon; it arrests the sun in its course, rules over all gods and opens and shuts the storehouses of rain. It unlocks the cabinet of the womb and quenches the violence of fire; it stops the mouths of lions and reconciles our suffering and weak faculties with the violence of torment and violence and of persecution; it pleases God and supplies all our need." **~ Jeremy Taylor**

"The secret of prayer is prayer in secret."
~ Wellington Boone

"Much time spent with God is the secret of all successful praying... Our short prayers owe their point and efficiency to the long ones that have preceded them..." ~ **E.M. Bounds**

"If I fail to spend two hours in prayer each morning, the devil gets the victory through the day. I have so much business that I cannot get on without spending three hours daily in prayer."
~ **Martin Luther**

"When the church of God is aroused to its obligation and duties and right faith to claim what Christ has promised... 'all things whatsoever' – a revolution will take place."
~ **John Foster**

"In the divine order, ministry to the Lord comes before ministry to men. Out of the ministry to the Lord, the Holy Spirit brings forth the direction and the power needed for effective ministry to men." ~ **Derek Prince**

"To be silent is to give consent. If you're silent, then God will be silent. But if you'll start praying, God will start moving. If you'll start speaking, God will start speaking."
~ **Jentezen Franklin**

"He that has prayed well has studied well." ~ **Martin Luther**

"The conflict is about the primacy of prayer. Defeat and victory lie in this one thing... If prayer is put first, then God is put first, and victory is assured." ~ **E.M. Bounds**

"God rules the world and His church through the prayers of His people." ~ **Andrew Murray**

"The story of every great Christian achievement is the history of answered prayer." ~ **E.M. Bounds**

"God does nothing but in answer to believing prayer."
~ **John Wesley**

"A pulpit without a closet will always be a barren thing."
~ **E.M. Bounds**

"A prayerless ministry is the undertaker for all God's truth and for God's church." ~ **E.M. Bounds**

"A great evangelist has said that truth will move men but prayer will move God and we need a move of God."
~ **John Nichols**

"These are the sort of men and women needed in this modern day in the church. It is not educated men who are need for the times. It is not more money that is required. It is not more machinery, more organization, more ecclesiastical laws, but it is men and women who know how to pray, who can in prayer lay hold upon God and bring Him down to earth, and move Him to take hold of earth's affairs mightily and put life and power into the church and into all of it machinery."
~ **E.M. Bounds**

"The less I pray, the harder it gets; the more I pray, the better it goes." ~ **Martin Luther**

"Man is never so tall as when he kneels before God—never so great as when he humbles himself before God. And the man who kneels to God can stand up to anything."
~ Louis H. Evans

"Prayer doesn't get man's will done in Heaven; it gets God's will done on earth." **~ Ronald Dunn**

"Prayer is exhaling the spirit of man and inhaling the Spirit of God." **~ Edwin Keith**

"I am better or worse as I pray more or less."
~ E. Stanley Jones

"Prayer is not learned in the classroom but in the closet."
~ E.M. Bounds

(In reference to praying with Authority)
"God has given you jurisdiction over your world — under His authority of course. He wants you, not sin, demonic powers, negative circumstances, or any other outside force to govern it... God's ultimate intention is for you to rule your personal world and to partner with His other kids in ruling the world around you. You are a government official" **~ Dutch Sheets**

"Prayer moves the hand which moves the world."
~ John Aikman Wallace

"Time Spent on the knees in prayer will do more to remedy heart strain and nerve worry than anything else."
~ George David Stewart

"The gates of hell will not prevail against a praying church."
~ Cindy Jacobs

"No weeping saints, no weeping sinners." **~ Nancy Shavaz**

"The church holds the balance of power in world affairs… Even now, in this present throbbing moment, by means of her prayer power and the extent to which she uses it, the praying church is actually deciding the course of human events."
~ Paul Billheimer

"In God's economy, prayer is vital currency." **~ Tim Elmore**

"Prayer can do anything God can do." **~ E.M. Bounds**

"Prayer is like the Word of God. We don't read enough today for the entire week." **~ Dutch Sheets**

"Prayer is the slender nerve that moves the muscles of omnipotence." **~ David Moses Keen**

"To be a Christian without prayer is no more possible than to be alive without breathing." **~ Martin Luther King Jr.**

"Courage is fear that has said its prayers." **~ Dorothy Bernard**

"Pray, and let God worry." **~ Martin Luther**

"Trouble and perplexity drive me to prayer and prayer drives away perplexity and trouble." **~ Philip Melanchthen**

"The value of consistent prayer is not that He will hear us, but that we will hear Him." **~ William McGill**

"Prayer may not change things for you, but it for sure changes you for things." ~ **Samuel M. Shoemaker**

"We have to pray with our eyes on God, not on the difficulties." ~ **Oswald Chambers**

"Prayers not felt by us are seldom heard by God."
~ **Philip Henry**

"To pray is to change. Prayer is the central avenue God uses to transform us. If we are unwilling to change, we will abandon prayer..." ~ **Richard Foster**

"Is prayer your steering wheel or your spare tire?"
~ **Corrie Ten Boom**

"Of all the duties enjoined by Christianity none is more essential and yet more neglected than prayer."
~ **François Fénelon**

"Wishing will never be a substitute for prayer." ~ **Ed Cole**

"When a Christian shuns fellowship with other Christians the devil smiles. When he stops studying the Bible, the devil laughs. When he stops praying, the devil shouts for joy."
~ **Corrie Ten Boom**

"If you can't pray a door open, don't pry it open."
~ **Lyell Rader**

"There is nothing that makes us love a man so much as praying for him." ~ **William Law**

"Rich is the person who has a praying friend."
~ Janice Hughes

"Search for a person who claims to have found Christ apart from someone else's prayer, and your search may go on forever." **~ E. Bauman**

"No one's a firmer believer in the power of prayer than the devil; not that he practices it, but he suffers from it."
~ Guy H. King

"Talk less with men; talk more with God. Listen less to men; listen to the words of God." **~ Leonard Ravenhill**

"Prayer is the first thing, the second thing, the third thing necessary to a minister. Pray, then my dear brother; pray, pray, pray." **~ Edward Payson**

"If we would pray aright, the first thing we should do is to see to it that we really get an audience with God that we really get into His very presence. Before a word of petition is offered, we should have the definite consciousness that we are talking to God, and should believe that He is listening and is going to grant the thing that we ask of Him." **~ R. A. Torrey**

"Every great movement of God can be traced to a kneeling figure." **~ D. L. Moody**

"Men are God's method. The church is looking for better methods; God is looking for better men. What the church needs today is not more machinery or better, not new

organizations or more and novel methods, but men who the Holy Spirit can use—men of prayer, men mighty in prayer. The Holy Spirit does not come on machinery but on men. He does not anoint plans, but men—men of prayer." ~ **E. M. Bounds**

"Discernment is God's call to intercession, never to faultfinding." ~ **Corrie Ten Boom**

"Intercessory prayer might be defined as loving our neighbor on our knees." ~ **Charles Brent**

"Prayer is the acid test of devotion." ~ **Samuel Chadwick**

"In the divine order, ministry to the Lord comes before ministry to men." ~ **Derek Prince**

"I pray and I obey." ~ **Paul Yonggi Cho**

"Men ought always to pray and not to faint."
~ **Jesus of Nazareth**

Chapter 15

WEEKLY PRAYER SCHEDULE

The following guide is specifically designed to help you concentrate your daily prayers on one specific area in the life of your leader for each day of the week. They are created in the form of short topical prayers that target key areas of a minister's life. These prayers are also male gender specific but you can adapt them for female leaders as well. This is not an exhaustive prayer guide. In other words, be led of the Holy Spirit and allow His wisdom to inspire you as you pray; waiting and pausing frequently through each prayer for insight. Leaders: These prayers will also serve as a powerful template when you pray for yourself. Take full advantage of it. A summary of the weekly schedule is as follows:

SUNDAY — *Integrity*

MONDAY — *Favor*

TUESDAY — *Vision*

WEDNESDAY — *Health*

THURSDAY — *Protection*
FRIDAY — *Finances*
SATURDAY — *Family*

SUNDAY — Integrity

"So he shepherded them according to the integrity of his heart, and guided them with his skillful hands."
~ Psalms 78:72 NASB

Lord, firmly root _____ in Your love. May he give no foothold to the enemy in his life. Grant him a heartfelt desire to live what he preaches. Help him shun the very appearance of evil and may he be in private what he proclaims in public. Divert him from all distractions and opportunities to participate in sinful and reproachable activities. Protect his reputation and let his noble character be seen by all. Give his enemies no opportunity to falsely accuse or malign him. Make him a powerful role model exemplifying holiness. Reveal any impure motives in his life and purge them. When he fails, help him quickly repent. May he be disciplined in his soul to avoid all selfish ambition. Help him to avoid the pitfalls of pride and arrogance and may humility be the benchmark of his life and ministry.

Holy Spirit, endorse _____'s ministry with Your power and let him stand out in all he does. May his work be of the most excellent and notable quality. Fill him with your wisdom and strengthen him in His inner man. Never allow him to minister in His own abilities. Grant him supernatural power to enact and enforce your kingdom on earth. Let all who experience his ministry know that they have truly been in the presence of God. May the gifts of the Holy Spirit powerfully rest and manifest in _____'s ministry. Help him not depend on past experiences but rely on you for each new and unique opportunity. Fill his heart with Your insight. Give him deep spiritual revelation, intellectual understanding and practical application of the Word of God. Grant him clear prophetic discernment regarding future events. Help him to be sensitive to the situations of others and give him creative solutions to solving conflicts that arise. May he clearly speak the things you are saying and showing to him (Acts 4:40).

If _____ falls into sin help him to admit it, humble himself under God proven leadership and take the necessary steps toward restoration. Help him to run to You, fall on Your forgiveness and receive Your abundant Grace. Remind him that you have never left him and never will. Remove any further condemnation and help him continue to walk through the healing process until it's completion.

MONDAY — Favor

"Let the favor of the Lord our God be upon us and confirm for us the work of our hands; Yes, confirm the work of our hands.'
~ Psalms 90:17 NASB

"Praising God and having favor with all the people. And the Lord was adding to their number day by day those who were being saved." ~ **Acts 2:47 NASB**

Heavenly Father, grant _____ such strong favor with man that even his enemies are at peace with him. May all who are influenced by his ministry come to a saving knowledge of Jesus Christ as Lord. Give his congregation teachable spirits and open hearts. Send Your ministering angels to watch over them in all their ways. Help them to be wise, strong and pure and be living testimonies of the effects of his ministry. May they be supportive and responsive to the ministry with love, prayers, encouragement and finances. Give them a desire for the things of God more than any unnecessary and ineffective traditions they may otherwise cling to. Help them to be open to new and genuine moves of God. May they refuse to dispense and receive gossip. Protect them from all deluding influences and guard them from wolves in sheep's clothing. Let revival spring forth in their lives.

Lord, make _____ a leader of leaders. Grant him double honor and esteem among all who cross his path. Enable him to relate to each member of his staff, building them up in their calling and purpose. Help them to remain unified and sensitive to the Holy Spirit. May they be supportive of one another. Help his staff esteem one another more highly than themselves and use wisdom to communicate clearly without misunderstanding. Let no weapon formed against them to prosper. Help them to work together cordially and efficiently and be honest in their relationships with one another. May they remain faithfully committed to serve and willing to go the extra mile when called upon. Inspire them to be more creative and productive than ever before.

Heavenly Father, help _____ communicate effectively and boldly. Prepare the hearts of the people to receive his ministry. Save, heal, deliver and fill them with miracle working power. Prevent Satan from stealing the Word that has been planted in their hearts. Send your deep conviction into their hearts by the power of the Holy Spirit and cause them not to hesitate even one second in responding to the clarion call of salvation and dedicated service. Let no person go unchanged.

TUESDAY — Vision

"Then the LORD answered me and said, "Record the vision and inscribe it on tablets that the one who reads it may run." ~
Habakkuk 2:2 NASB

Holy Spirit, help _____ be sensitive to Your voice clearly discerning between Your thoughts and his own thoughts. Be the initiator for all vision. May his goals be those that You have ordained for His life and help him to keep his "eye on the prize." Help the people receive the vision and be patience until its fulfillment. Provide more than enough resources for the vision (provision for the vision). Place a "wall of fire" around the administration of the vision (Zechariah 2:5). Raise up willing vessels to help carry out the vision. Grant him discernment and solutions against the tactics of the enemy that would delay the vision from coming forth in God's timing and shut the mouths of those who would speak against it. Surround him with Godly counsel and help him to be open to correction and realignment. Help him to receive constructive guidance from the wisdom of other key leaders appreciatively and without offense. May he never seek to advance his own agenda but rather the building of Your kingdom and the lives of others.

WEDNESDAY — Health

"Beloved, I pray that in all respects you may prosper and be in good health, just as your soul prospers."
~ I Thessalonians 5:23 NASB

Lord, grant _____ divine health in every area of his life. Refresh him from all fatigue and renew his strength as he waits on You. Help him to apply wisdom and self-control in eating, exercise and sleep habits. Loose him from every unhealthy compulsion. Help him define clear boundaries for his life and teach him when and how to say, "No." Give him supernatural strength to accomplish every meaningful and necessary task and give him wisdom to eliminate all unproductive and wasteful activities. Heal him from all sickness and prevent him from developing any future illness that would impede him from running the race you have set before him. May he radiate joy and attract others to the Lord through appearance, actions and gentle and charming speech. Remove the spirit of unhealthy competition in his life and let graciousness exude from him. Teach him to be polite in all his mannerisms yet all the bolder in his proclamation of the gospel. Let mercy and compassion freely flow from his life. May he be a peacemaker, seeking to restore broken relationships, especially where he is at fault. May he exemplify humility rather than superiority. Grant him a spirit of cooperation. Help him to recognize all negative attitudes and motives, and give him insight to properly deal with them.

THURSDAY — Protection

"The LORD is my rock and my fortress and my deliverer, My God, my rock, in whom I take refuge; my shield and the horn of my salvation, my stronghold." ~ **Psalms 18:2 NASB**

Heavenly Father, send angels to guard over _____'s family and his property. Grant safe passage to all who enter and leave his home. Help him to surrender the fight to you. Foil all attacks and traps of the enemy. Hide and preserve him from trouble, surrounding him with songs of deliverance (Psalms 32:7). Make him aware of the schemes of the enemy as necessary. Go before him making the crooked place straight, shattering bronze doors and cutting through iron bars (Psalms 107:16; Isaiah 45:2). Help him to refuse to be materialistic boastful, proud, abusive, rebellious, ungrateful, unholy, hateful, unforgiving, slanderous, impulsive, brutal, uncaring, synical, treacherous, rash, conceited, and obsessed with pleasure more than with God (2 Timothy 3:2-4). Prevent him from giving in to the lust of the flesh, the lust of the eyes and the pride of life (1 John 2:16). Holy Spirit, keep him from being led astray into error by false doctrines and false prophets (Matthew 24:24). Also prevent him from preaching error. Guard him from hypocrisy and religious spirits, antichrist, antichurch, unholy spirits and demonically inspired counterfeit signs and wonders. Surround him with Godly people who will stand in his defense and help insulate him from his assailants.

Lord, guard _____ from all principalities, powers, rulers of darkness and spiritual wickedness in high places that come against him. Protect him against any occult activity, curses, witchcraft, divination and sorcery. I bind the strongman and cast him out (Psalms 149; Matthew 12:29; 16:19). Cancel all demonic assignments sent against him (1 John 3:8). Foil the signs of false prophets and make fools of the diviners (Isaiah 44:25). Unleash fury upon his adversaries. Let his enemies fall into their own traps while he walks safely by without harm (Psalms 23:5; 141:9-10) Avenge all wrong done to him and his family (Psalms 35 & 37). Restore what the enemy tried to steal, kill and destroy. Release him from the need to defend himself against his opponents and help him to trust You to vindicate him. Help him to pursue righteousness, faith, love and peace with all men so that he doesn't cause his enemies to further retaliate. Grant your servant perseverance in the presence of opposition. Help him to obey You no matter how high or difficult the cost and give him a willing heart even in the most severe circumstances. Remove the "quit option" from his vocabulary. Help him to boldly speak Your word regardless of any adversity he faces.

FRIDAY — Finances

"And my God will supply all your needs according to His riches in glory in Christ Jesus." ~ **Philippians 4:19 NASB**

Father, cause _____ to abound in prosperity and effectively and efficiently manage every area of his life and ministry. Help him to recognize all unproductive strategies and be open to change. May he be a wise steward of his time and resources. Lord, help Him to keep accurate records of all vital accounts and send highly qualified people to assist him in solid administration. Help him to operate on a planned budget with guidance and strict accountability. Stir up supporters for the ministry who will be obedient and extravagant in their giving and bless them for their generosity. Multiply every investment he has made into your kingdom. Give him the desires of his heart because he delights in God. I thank You that all his needs are met according to Your riches in Glory. Restore every loss even where it was due to his own ignorance and negligence. Break the curse from his increase and rebuke the devourer. Cause his prosperity to abound in so that he will have an abundance for every good work.

SATURDAY – Family

"For where envying and strife is there is confusion and every evil work." ~ **James 3:16 KJV**

Lord, create an atmosphere of unity and mutual understanding within the family. Heal any unresolved conflict and let Your presence fill every facet of their home life. Prevent any resentment when sacrifice for the ministry is required. Help the whole family embrace the vision of the ministry as one and be vitally active in it. Help them to plan and participate in prayer and devotions. Cause each member to operate their unique, God-given gifts and talents. Make their home warm, hospitable, peaceable and irresistible to others. Make their place of dwelling a sanctuary of healing and restoration to all who cross their threshold and enter their doors. Make theirs a model family and home to even the most prominent members of their community.

Marriage

Heavenly Father, completely meet the emotional needs of _____ and his wife so they will not have unrealistic expectations from one another. Help them to maintain pure, effective communication and be sympathetic listeners to one another. Give them ample opportunity for uninterrupted quality time with each other (spiritually, physically and emotionally). Help them recognize that they are a team. May they encourage and help one another, considering each other's need above their own. Help them to be fiercely loyal and faithful to one another. May they live complementary with one another, not competitively where jealousy and envy exist. Help them discern each other's needs (emotional physical, material and spiritual) and to meet that need where possible. May they manifest the fruit of the Spirit in their marriage. Heal them from past regrets and resentments. Release them from unfair expectations of one another. Help them to hear your voice individually and as a marriage. Give them strength to overcome the pressures and stress of ministry. Help them resist living up to other people's expectations and be released to be the unique individuals God has created them to be. Help them to appreciate and focus each other's strengths and to forgive and forbear their weaknesses. Remove all strife within their union and break the yoke of accusation and quarrelling. Help them resist the urge to place blame on one another but serve one another. Make theirs a model marriage and a powerful example of the love of Christ to all who come into contact with them.

Children

Father, I confess that _____'s children have the reverential awe of the Lord. Help them to demonstrate love, patience, understanding and loyalty toward their parents, family and ministry. Help them choose righteous friends and send them Godly relationships. Deliver them from ungodly ties (past, present, future). Keep all negative influences from entering their lives. Keep them in Your circle of safety. Give them a desire to participate in the ministry at the level You have called them and prevent resentment from arising.

Help them to be flexible and adapt to change in ministry, especially where moving is involved. Set them free from expectations put on them by others that are not in line with God's will. Help them clearly hear God's voice individually and respond obediently. May they never be a disgrace to their home and church. When they are involved in any ungodly, indiscriminate, inordinate or rebellious activity, expose them in a proper way so they cannot hide their deeds in the darkness. Bring to light any shameful activity in an appropriate manner so they may be accountable, repent and be fully restored. In every case, remove the stigma that others put on them and let them stand apart as exemplary children. Cause them to excel in every area of their lives and grant them favor with their peers and leaders.

When _____'s children fall into sin, let them experience Your unfailing love. Cause them to run into Your arms of mercy knowing that You will receive them with no condemnation never casting them away. Let them have a deep conviction that You will never leave them or forsake them. Let Your Grace surround them and remind them of their bright future! Set them completely free and let them live as if they never sinned at all!

Chapter 16

MONTHLY PRAYER SCHEDULE

The following Monthly Prayer Schedule was adapted and revised from Dr. R.J. Krejcir, Into Thy Word Ministries, www.intothyword.org ©2005. This schedule can be powerfully incorporated as you fervently pray for your entire church and it's God appointed leadership.

DAY 1: Pray that your leader realizes that his inheritance and hope is in God's incomparable and incredible great power (Galatians 1:12; Ephesians 1:18-19; Philippians 3:10).

DAY 2: Pray that your leader and his Staff become more surrendered and poured out to Christ, so he can have spiritual breakthroughs by seeking the mind of Christ and the Spirit's leading (1 Corinthians 2:16; Galatians 2:20-21).

Day 3: Pray that your leader continues to take hold of a growing, consistent walk with Christ through a steadfast devotional life and prayer. Pray he realizes and allows Christ to work through him, as he grows stronger in faith, maturity, and love (Psalms 16:8-11; 73:28; Romans 8:31; 2 Peter. 1:5-7).

Day 4: Pray that all of the leadership will exhibit good Christian character and integrity with all of their relationships and dealings in life (Micah 6:8).

Day 5: Pray that your leader's family will be cared for and respected and receive good consideration, so they may also grow, as they are usually misunderstood, under-appreciated, and ignored or overworked. Pray that the leader's staff be committed to their families with authentic love and care, that they will be strong and learn in the midst of trials, their homes a refuge and haven of rest and not be condescending or withdrawing from their own families (Psalms 91:9-15; Philippians 4:19; 1 Peter 2:23).

DAY 6: Pray for discernment in exposing any plans and attack of the enemy against your leader. Ask Christ to protect them as they win victories against the enemy (Ephesians 6:11-12, 16; Colossians 2:6-8; 1 Peter 3:12).

DAY 7: Pray for an increase of vitality, renewal and Godly vision for your leader so that the ministry can be revitalized and galvanized for God's Kingdom and purpose (Isaiah 61:3; Romans 12).

DAY 8: Pray that your leader will be willing and able to authentically confess and repent of any wrong doing, false dependencies, misplaced ideas and loss of spiritual passion (Luke 13:1-3; Acts 2:38-39; Revelation 2:5-6).

DAY 9: Pray that your leader will commit to follow the Biblical mandate to support and encourage the other key leaders of the ministry (Ephesians 4:11-13; 1 Timothy 5:17-18; 1 Peter 5:1-2).

DAY 10: Pray against gossip, negative criticism, false expectations, unhealthy burdens, strife and weariness that will seek to invade your leader's life (Psalms 91:5-6, 11; Luke 10:19; Ephesians 4: 17, 32-5:1).

DAY 11: Pray that your leader will be full of Grace and forgiveness; that he be surrounded in an atmosphere of mutual honor, respect and encouragement, thereby, able to pour out genuine hospitality to those in need (Romans 15:4-6; 2 Thessalonians 2:16-17).

DAY 12: Pray that your leader commits to a healthy understanding, wisdom and accounting and handling of finances to better receive God's blessings (Proverbs 3:9-10; 1 Corinthians 9:15-18).

DAY 13: Pray that your leader will have more than enough energy, strength, and endurance to serve with excellence by the power of the Spirit and the support of the people. Pray that he recognizes his need to receive abundant Grace that he may lead well (Philippians 4:13; Romans 5:17).

DAY 14: Pray that your leader will receive healing, and release forgiveness and reconciliation for any misplaced expectations, criticism, ungrateful attitudes, flawed thinking, grief, hurts, and abuse (Isaiah 61:3; Mark 11:22-24, 2 Corinthians 10:3-5; Ephesians 4:32-5:1; Philippians 4:19).

DAY 15: Pray that your leader will receive only God's direction and vision so that the needs of the people and ministry are met beyond what the he is able to provide (Psalms 119:9-12; Matthew 18:20).

DAY 16: Pray that your leader can provide what is needed to develop the people around him into authentic disciples of Christ, who are learning, growing and producing fruit and in turn making more disciples (Proverbs 19:23; Malachi 3:11; Matthew 28:18-20; John. 15:16; Galatians 5:22-23)

DAY 17: Pray that the spirit and practice of humility is utilized and practiced through your leader, and that false humility does not take root (1 Peter 5:5-7).

DAY 18: Pray that pride does not set in with your leader and his staff (Psalms 10:4; Proverbs 8:13).

DAY 19: Pray that your leader commits to place focus on the supremacy of Christ and be completely dependent upon Him (Galatians 6:14; Colossians 1:15-17).

DAY 20: Pray that your leader provides real Biblical help and counseling from God's wisdom and Word to those in need (Isaiah 61:3).

DAY 21: Pray that your leader will give Christ authentic adoration, praise, impassioned worship and glory in private times. Pray that he never treats worship as entertainment (Galatians 6:14).

DAY 22: Pray that your leader receives accountability seriously and humbly, cultivating and pursuing healthy relationships for his own protection and promotion (Galatians 6: 1-10; Ephesians 5:21).

DAY 23: Pray that the Word of God will never be compromised, cheapened or toned-down; rather be delivered in confidence with power, conviction, clarity, boldness, with love and in truth (Acts 6:4; Colossians 1:28; 1 Timothy 2:1-2; 2 Timothy 2:15).

DAY 24: Pray that your leader will have discernment to seek God's leading and direction, properly administrating passing trends, traditions, personal agendas or anything that is not from the Spirit and Word. Pray that your leader will prioritize what is important and precious and what is not (Isaiah 6; 2 Corinthians 11:14; 2 Timothy 3:5; 1 John. 4:1; Revelation 4).

DAY 25: Pray that God protects your leader from falling into sin and misdirection and he will have the willingness and boldness to flee and confront it (Proverbs 19:23; 1 Peter 1:16).

DAY 26: Pray that your leader will draw near to Christ, pursue holiness, and passionately preserve the desire for God's presence in his life (Leviticus 6:9-13; Acts 1:14; 1 Thessalonians 5:17; James 4:7-8).

DAY 27: Pray that your leader remains faithful and diligent to good stewardship so all his financial needs will met (Psalm. 91:15-16; Philippians 4:19).

DAY 28: Pray that negative thinking, stress, being overwhelmed, the ways of the world, the tyranny of the urgent, being overcommitted, over busyness, fatigue, compromise, pressures, overworked, under-appreciated, misunderstandings, and stress not have access to your leader (John 14:1; Acts 6:2-4; 2 Corinthians 10:3-5; Ephesians 4:17).

DAY 29: Pray that you leader will have the wisdom to cultivate unity so that the ministry is binding to the love of Christ and the work of the Kingdom is promoted and advanced (2 Chronicles 30:12; Psalms 133:1; Romans 15:5).

DAY 30: Pray that the people will be willing and able to avail themselves to support the ministry with grateful hearts, hands and words. Pray that they recognize the gifting, calling and necessity of their leader and that he is accountable to God (Matthew 9:37; Acts 14; 1 Timothy 3:17-15; 5:22-23).

DAY 31: Pray that your leader commits to pray for the ministry, staff, key missionaries, those in need, community and other important related issues (Acts 1:14; 16:16; 1 Thessalonians 5:17).

Chapter 17

FAQ'S ABOUT PRAYER

This section has been provided to serve primarily as a resource for those who have a burden for their leaders but are in beginning stages of formulating and developing their philosophy on prayer. This will probably be review information for more seasoned Christians, yet hopefully will discover it to be helpful as well. One of the Biblical responsibilities of ministry is to equip the saints and thus this section has been provided. There are many questions when it comes to prayer. I have found however that many succumb to the trifling of debate in excuse to avoid prayer altogether. It is ironic that people spend more time inquiring about prayer rather than getting to the praying. Be certain, it is not as necessary to have a theology of prayer as much as it is a *kneeology* of prayer.

Therefore, vital to seeking God is a true desire to understand the matter. When our searching is birthed from a sincere desire to know God's heart on prayer, it will result in a powerful prayer life. By this, we can expect to receive Heaven's munitions. Therefore, I have attempted to provide a brief summary of the most frequently asked questions asked about prayer and give credence to the answers. Once again, keep in mind that asking questions about prayer is beneficial only as it results in the application and regular practice of *asking God* in prayer.

What is Prayer?

Prayer is simply relating and communicating to God through authentic conversation. It is both speaking to Him and listening to His thoughts towards us. It is releasing and responding. It is expressing through words our heart's desire for God's perfect will to be revealed and enacted through our lives. It is the ability to implore the mighty hand of God into our affairs and witness, first hand, His authority established through our lives upon the earth. We can do no better thing than commune with infinite love and conscript ultimate power. To know God intimately and to encounter His presence expressly: this is the privilege and purpose of prayer. To avoid prayer is to refuse to employ His power and wisdom in our lives (James 4:2).

Do I have to pray?

The question isn't *should we pray* but rather *why shouldn't we pray?* Why wouldn't we desire to avail all that God is and can be through the collaboration of humanity and deity? We don't have to eat or drink but the absence of such implores a disastrous effect. When prayer becomes the life breath of our being we will ascend into heights otherwise unknown had we remained silent to the call to pray (Jeremiah 33:3).

Should I pray if God already knows what I need?

Often we are not sure of what we really need until we hear our own thoughts conceived audibly. Meditation is not prayer or else it wouldn't be distinguished as such in God's Word. When we speak we bring to light the inadequacies of our own desires and can separate them into the necessary or unnecessary. Do we have needs that are prideful, unimportant to the matter or even destructive? Often we don't know the answer to these until we bring voice to what's in our heart. Do we have thoughts that can't be articulated? When we speak it is uncanny how much easier it is to prioritize the mundane for the urgent. God knows our thoughts but often we don't. A principle to adhere to in prayer is that our perceptions remain cloudy in our thoughts until we make them clear with our words.

Obedient praying brings hidden things to light in order that we can make sense of them and pray aright. It is not necessary to pray grammatically correct. God knows well our heart's *intent* before we formalize the *content.* The main reason for the Biblical precedent to pray is to make verbally known our requests before God in order that our minds be established in peace at His ability to perform His promises (Philippians 4:6-7).

How long should I pray?

The answer to this depends on our pride, inadequacy, urgency, contempt, humility, dependence and all other attitudes and emotional dealings. Unanswered prayer often drives us to extremes. However, no matter the amount of time, God hears us the moment we entreat Him (Daniel 10:12). The fervency and frequency of our prayers do not determine the effectiveness. Rather the outcome of prayer is totally dependent upon our faith and knowing that God hears us. When we know He hears us we know we have the petitions we have asked (1 John 5:14-15). Also, knowing that we are righteous based on Christ's finished work apart from our works gives us courage in the face of condemnation. We then approach God confidently knowing our prayers are heard. It is not our faithfulness that determines answered prayer, but rather through God's faithfulness alone that we have what we have asked for.

Does God hear my prayers if I have sin in my life?

Psalms 66:18 NIV says, *"If I had cherished sin in my heart, the Lord would not have listened."* The distinction here is *"cherished sin."* We all struggle with sin issues in certain areas of our lives. This is certain. However, if we regularly cooperate with the Holy Spirit (even though we are not victorious in every area) our prayers will be heard and taken into account. I've also strongly believed that God speaks to those who obey Him the quickest.

To be certain, Grace covers our inadequacies but we must understand that pride regarding sins undealt with will hinder our prayers. We will always be stuck at the last point of our disobedience. God is more concerned with the condition of the person praying than He is for the conditions being prayed for. Prayer often reveals or even amplifies what is hidden in our own lives. When we allow His Grace to transform us, it will indeed make us more effective 'pray-*ers*.' God's Grace alone is sufficient to cover us but we must submit our disobedience to God and allow that Grace to change us. A life filled with pride will pray *pridefully*. Thus we must allow Grace to purge us so we may pray in accordance with God's will. If God's will isn't being done in us how then can we pray, *"Thy will be done on earth?"* (Luke 11:2)

What time of day is best to pray?

The matter of when and how we should pray is not as important as the matter of whom is praying and what is being prayed. The *what* often determines the *when.* The urgency of the moment often produces the frequency of prayer. More important than the time is the desire in which prayer is preceded. However, for many, morning is the time when our thoughts are most clear (I have elaborated more on this previously in Chapter 7).

I once heard a proverb on prayer declaring we must seek God during the early hours when the dew is most latent on the ground, for it is in the high heat of noon when the moisture has dissipated. We've all ignored the gentle prompting to pray in the morning and whence the day in full motion, we find ourselves swiftly tumbling downstream in its uncontrollable current. When we prioritize prayer in the schedule of our day, it helps us to attain proper perspective and focus on everything that follows. If you jump on a horse without first firmly grasping the reigns it will run amuck flinging you forlorn into the rocks. That's how I think of prayer: first things first – *grabbing the reigns* of my day as it were. Another reason for quiet devotional reflection in the morning is it is better to get God's word on the matter first rather than someone else's. Be certain that you will hear what others have to say throughout your day. Therefore, it is better to filter all the thoughts and words that will potentially bombard you through the Word God has first spoken to your heart. When God speaks first all other opposing view points are silenced. His voice dominates all conversations. God's *first mention* drowns out our misguided intentions and satan's evil inventions.

What if I don't have time to pray?

Again, this is not the appropriate question. The question should be *"What am I doing with the time I have?"* Priorities are the greatest influencers of our lives. They determine our choices and those choices create our comfort or our pain. If we were honest with ourselves we would discover that most problems stem from misappropriated priorities. One way to discover our true priorities is to take an honest look at our use of time. What we give the most time to reveals what is most important to us. The difference between success and failure is the use of time. Simply put; we are a byproduct of our use of time. I have difficulty believing we don't have time for God in prayer (at some level). God has given everyone the same 24-hours. Priority precedes order. How we order our lives is directly related to our priorities. If we say God is first, He will be prioritized in our daily schedule. And rest assured, if we prioritize the things of God (I.e. worship, prayer, Bible study) then our lives will reflect the quality of that decision. The key is consistency. Here's the prayer math: Subtracted self-reliance + Added minutes in prayer = MULTIPLIED RESULTS. The marvelous paradox is the more time we spend with God, the more time we will WANT to spend with Him.

How can I hear God while I'm praying?

In all actuality, God's response to us is much louder than words. Most of the time we can't hear, as it were, with our natural ear. That's because the things of God are spiritually discerned (1 Corinthians 2:14). Prayer is God's Spirit communicating to our spirit. The book of Revelation calls it having an *"ear to hear."* (Revelation 2:7) Our sensitivity is heightened on every level (emotional, physical, mental, spiritual, etc.) when we engage God in genuine, heartfelt, prayer. We hear things with our ears all the time but most often forget them. That's why a verbal reply from God is insufficient. When God hears a true heart cry from us, be sure that we will clearly hear Him, feel Him, know Him and sense Him when He speaks...

"In my distress I called upon the LORD, and cried to my God for help; He heard my voice out of His temple, and my cry for help before Him came into His ears. Then the earth shook and quaked; and the foundations of the mountains were trembling and were shaken." ~ **Psalms 18:6 NASB**

Do I need a special place for prayer?

Special places of meeting are endearing to our hearts. We take vacations, go on dates, eat out and go on walks in these special gathering places. If I were to ask you if you had a special place where you regularly meet with God could you show me where it was? In days gone by these places of prayer were called the "secret place." As I afore mentioned earlier in this book, my late grandmother had such a place where she prayed every day. It was a red velvet swivel chair (which still sits in my Mom and Dad's house today). I remember seeing her leaning back in that chair so often and crying, worshiping and praying. History was changed in that chair. Although it is not as important as the praying itself, "secret places" where we gather can garner significant praying from us. Also, we know that our secret place is Jesus Himself. Yet Jesus himself often withdrew to pray in quiet secluded places where he could be alone with His Father (Luke 5:16). We don't HAVE to have a regular *place* of prayer. The key is that we should regularly pray. However, if you pray regularly, you may find yourself meeting with God in the same place often. It will become the secret place that draws you to the Father's heart often. And it is in that place that you will alter the course of your future!

What is the best posture for prayer?

The Bible gives us many examples of the physical positions we can take when praying. We can walk, stand, kneel, raise our hands, fall on our faces and even lay in bed. Our posturing in prayer often determines the level or intensity in which we pray. For instance, when we intently stretch our hands upward, we tend to focus more intently on the matter at hand. When we kneel, it naturally draws an attitude of submission. When we fall prostrate on our faces it seems easier to completely surrender to God.

Our physical posture in prayer has a profound way of spiritually posturing us before the Lord. However, more important than our physical posture is the posture of our heart. Are we truly yielded to God's will when we pray? This is the question. A better question to ask ourselves is, what will make my praying more effective and often the Holy Spirit will lead us in the corresponding posturing. And if our heart is yielded to God we will follow the Spirit's prompting to obey in the posturing. After all, if we can't obey Him during prayer how can we think we will obey Him post prayer?

Is there a special gift of prayer?

Some think that it isn't their *calling* pray; that prayer is a ministry position or title. Nothing could be farther from the truth. Although some have accepted the position to lead prayer groups or pastor a prayer ministry, it is the calling and responsibility of every believer to commune with God. Again, if prayer is viewed as only a ministry and not also as an opportunity to develop our relationship with God, we will miss the mark. For instance, if we go too long without talking to our wives, children and friends, there will be a natural distance in the relationship. Thus it is with prayer. We mustn't perceive that prayer is for some while not for others. Nowhere in Scripture does it support the concept of prayer as a spiritual gift. Paul instructed the entire Church as Colossae, *"Devote yourselves to prayer, being watchful and thankful."* (Colossians 4:2)

Can I read my prayers?

The answer: ABSOLUTELY! Often when I pray I open the Psalms and read them, pausing often to meditate and pray (in my own words) the thoughts of King David (who knew so well how to call out to God). The prayers of the greatest men and women of God are scattered all through out the pages of scripture and we can often read their own words as models to effective praying. God's Word is full of encouragement, faith and revelation, which we desperately need when we pray. Scriptures are filled with lamentations, praises, prayer strategies, meditative reflections, pleas of desperation, revelatory insights and even outlines to prayer. Jesus Himself taught us a simple outline to pray, which the church has used for ages to unlock the storehouses of Heaven. Reading prayers are a powerful way to stay focused and pray God's will. After all, if it's in the Word of God then it is the will of God. However, it is important to remember to be led by the Spirit when we pray and speak from our own heart sincere words that communicate our wants, needs, concerns and petitions (Philippians 4:6). In all of this we must be certain, God will always lead us to His Word in prayer.

How do I keep my mind focused when pray?

Often our mind wanders when we pray. Fact is, we can't always prevent thoughts from entering our mind but we can choose what to do with them. We can't stop the birds from flying over our heads but we can prevent them from nesting in our hair. Therefore, the best way to keep thoughts from taking over our times of prayer is to keep a pen and paper handy. I think of this as praying the *"write-way."* A prayer journal is the most practical way to do this. Our greatest Biblical examples wrote their prayers and we are still praying them today. Once our thoughts *land* on paper they usually leave the preoccupation of our minds until later opportunity for application. We should also make note that our thoughts aren't always interruptions. Often, our mental musings are simply reminders from the Holy Spirit regarding the things we need give attention to. However, many times our *mind battles* are the very points of prayer. However, we don't have to get our minds "right" before we pray. It is during prayer that the Holy Spirit helps us *get* our minds right! When we enter the presence of God through prayer, we should avoid using many words (Psalms 46:10; Ecclesiastes 5:2) and allow the Holy Spirit to quiet our anxious thoughts and speak first. Many times we *fray* instead of pray. However, when this is difficult for us to do, we can freely approach God with whatever is on our mind and surrender it to the Lord. God's presence stills all our worry, bringing peace and resolve to every dilemma.

Chapter 18

TOGETHER WE WIN!

"First of all, then, I urge that entreaties and prayers, petitions and thanksgivings, be made on behalf of all men, for kings AND ALL WHO ARE IN AUTHORITY, that we may lead a tranquil and quiet life in all godliness and dignity. This is good and acceptable in the sight of God our Savior." ~ **1 Timothy 2:1-3**

My network of intercessors is called Worldwide Intercessors Newtork (W.I.N.). The slogan for my team is *"Together We W.I.N.!"* Nothing is as powerful as a unified team of intercessors. To this I have written this book in hopes that I can inspire, equip and release other W.I.N. cells across the globe for the sake of holding up our leaders through the ministry of strategic intercession. Therefore, for the remainder of my life and ministry I am passionately dedicated to pray for and to help raise up and end-time army of intercessors to pray for their leaders. So what about you? God is ready to empty His ammunition vaults into the hands of His loyal and trustworthy secret service prayer agents. It must be one of the primary callings of the believer to pray for their spiritual leaders. Paul tells us that first prayers must be prayed for Kings and for ALL who are in authority. This includes our spiritual leaders who are set in positions of Godly authority who watch over us. Andrew Murray from His book *The Secret of Intercession* says:

> *"Let all intercessors who are seeking to enter more deeply into their blessed work give a larger place to the ministry, whether of their own church or of other churches. Let them plead with God for specific individuals and for special circles. Let them continue in prayer and watch therein, that ministers may be men of power, men of prayer and men full of the Holy Spirit. Oh, friends, pray for the ministry... Intercession is indeed a divine reality. Without it, the church loses one of its chief beauties as well as the joy and the power of the Spirit life for achieving great things for God. Without it, the command to preach the Gospel to every creature can never be carried out. Without it, there is no power for the church to recover from her sickly, feeble life and conquer the world. And in the life of the believer, minister or member; there can be no entrance into the abundant life and joy of daily fellowship with God, except as he takes his place among God's elect—the watchmen and remembrancers of God who cry to Him*

day and night. Church of Christ, awake, awake! Listen to the call, "Pray without ceasing." Take no rest, and give God no rest... May God help us to know and to fulfill our calling!"

Are you committed to doing whatever it takes to ensure that your leaders are covered in prayer? Spiritual leaders cannot step out into the *great unknown* without grasping onto the *God of the unknown.* All the promises of God must be apprehended by faith and spoken in prayer to the realization of God's will to be done on earth as it is in Heaven. As you ponder the words in this book, you should be confident that they will be forever grateful to you for your love and unending support in prayer. Your leaders need you, whether they want to admit it or not. Don't wait for your leader to make a special request for prayer. You've already been given a formal invitation from the God of the universe to pray for your leaders. Deep down, most leaders know that their hope of success of making God's glory known to men is prayer. Any great man or woman of God will tell you that rise or fall of their ministry is equal only to the strength or weakness of the prayers of the saints. Upon looking at the statue of a famous man, Oliver Cromwell once made this profound remark: *"Make my statue kneeling; for thus I came to glory."* For all who have heard the voice of the Spirit to join ranks to pray and intercede for your leaders I commend you and all of Heaven applauds you. All things are possible with God! May He move every mountain before you as you plow the road to Heaven's gate in prayer for your leaders. Your reward and your leader's reward will be very great! When we pray together we W.I.N. Together we W.I.N.!

ABOUT THE AUTHOR

For nearly three decades Tony Sutherland has served on staff in the local church as well as traveled extensively around the world stirring in hearts everywhere a passion for God's presence and a powerful Grace awakening through his music, teaching and preaching. Tony has captured the unique ability to effectively reach a wide diversity of people in today's church. His dynamic ministry style crosses denominational and cultural barriers impacting children, youth, young adult, middle age and seniors. Congregations large and small are refreshed by his passion for Jesus. Along with his busy traveling schedule, Tony has served on staff as a Worship Leader at Free Chapel's main campus in Gainesville, GA under the ministry of Pastor Jentezen Franklin for the past ten years.

Having over a quarter-century combined experience in various ministry areas including: worship, youth & children, church planting, associate pastor, and an expansive itinerate ministry in evangelism and foreign missions (to name a few), Tony is well equipped to address the life of the local church on numerous levels.

Along with these, he has also ministered in hundreds of established and thriving churches as well as young, church plants around the world, consulting a plethora of pastors from every size congregation, cultural background, denomination and Christ-centered church movement. His extensive research and hands-on involvement in helping to develop church environments is an invaluable resource for growing ministries desiring to adopt a culture that is entirely Christ-centered with a Christ centered, Spirit-led paradigm.

Tony is also an accomplished songwriter having written songs with and for artists such as Israel Hougton, Micah Massey, Ricardo Sanchez, Ce Ce Winans, The Katinas, Mandisa, Phillips-Craig & Dean, Bishop Paul Morton, David & Nichole Binion, Ashmont Hill, Daryl Coley, Myron Butler, Ron Kenoly and many others.

Tony resides in the North Atlanta area with Sherri, his beautiful wife of 25 years and their two amazing children, Asher and Anna.

ENDNOTES

1. "Authority in Prayer (Praying with Power and Purpose)" E Dutch Sheets. Bethany House, ©2006.

2. "Fasting Forward" By Billy Wilson. Pathway Press, ©2005.

3. "How to Have a Prayer Ministry"" Charles E. Fuller Institu (Section on Intercession for Christian Leaders), ©1990.

4. "Intercessory Prayer" By Dutch Sheets. Regal Books, ©1996

5. "Let the Children Pray" by Esther Ilnisky. Regal (a division gospel Light), ©2000.

6. "Pivotal Praying" by John Hull & Tim Elmore. Thomas Nelso Publishers, ©2002.

7. "Possessing the Gates of the Enemy" By Cindy Jacot Chosen Books, ©1991.

8. "Prayers that Outwit the Enemy" By Chuck D. Pierce Rebecca Wagner Sytsema. Regal Books, ©2004

9. "Right People Right Place, Right Plan" by Jentezen Frankl Whitaker House, ©2007.

10. "Shaping History Through Prayer and Fasting" by Dere Prince. Whitaker House, ©1973.

11. "The Best of E.M. Bounds on Prayer." Baker book Hous Company, ©1981.

12. "The Hidden Power of Prayer and Fasting" By Mahesh Chavda. Destiny's Image, ©1998.

13. "The Pastor's Prayer Partners" ©Injoy Ministries (Section on Praying for My Leader)

14. "Total Forgiveness" by R.T. Kendall. Charisma House, ©2002.

15. "Sparkling Gems from the Greek" By Rick Renner. Teach All Nations, ©2003.

16. "How to Become a Prayer Warrior" Gospel Light Publications, ©2002 (Increase International)

17. "Fasting" By Jentezen Franklin. Charisma House, ©2008

18. 24-7 Prayer (www.24-7prayer.com)

19. Esther Network International (www.lcciwpb.com)

20. Friends of the Bridegroom (www.fotb.com)

21. Fusion Ministries Inc. (www.prayerbydesign.com)

22. Generals International (www.generals.org)

23. Houses of Prayer Everywhere (www.hopeministries.org)

24. Intercessors For America (www.ifa-usapray.org)

25. Intercessors International (www.intercessorsinternational.org)

26. Pray Magazine (www.navpress.com/magazines/pray!/)

27. Pray Today (www.pray-today.com)

28. Revival Resource Center (www.watchword.org)

29. "I Lift My Eyes" (www.psalm121.ca/prayer.html)

30. "Fire in My Bones" (www.godtube.com)

References for Ministry Burnout & Dropout

31. "Spirituality for Ministry" By Urban T. Holmes, San Francisco Harper & Row Publishers, ©1982.

32. "Mad Church Disease (Overcoming the Burnout Epidemic)" By Anne Jackson, Zondervan, ©2009.

33. "Pastors at Greater Risk." By H.B. London Jr. and Neil B. Wiseman. Regal Books, ©2003.

34. "Taking a Break from the Lord's Work" NY Times, August 2010.

35. "Burnout for Pastors" By Scot McKnight, from London and Wiseman's Pastors at Greater Risk, ©2003

36. "Ministry burnout Statistics" By Alan Fadling (http://unhurriedtime.com/2009/06/03/ministry-burnout-stats/

37. "Pastor Dropout Rate" By John Mark Ministries (http://jmm.aaa.net.au/artiles/8084.htm)

38. "Statistics on Pastors (What is Going on with the Pastors in America?)" Dr. Richard J. Krejcir. (www.intothyword.org)

39. Focus on the Family (http://www.parsonage.org/)

40. http://theburnedoutpastor.com/stats.htm

41. www.acts29network.org, Mark Driscoll (post on July 2, 2007)

42. http://www.keepgodinamerica.com/statistics.asp

43. http://www.barna.org/search?q=church+decline

44. http://www.barna.org/search?q=church+attendance

45. http://churchsociety.org

46. http://www.keepgodinamerica.com/statistics.asp

47. *"7 Charismatic Characters Who Shouldn't Be On Your Ministry Team"* By J. Lee Grady, Charisma Magazine Online. © June 2014. (www.charismamag.com)

48. *"The Circle Maker"* By Mark Batterson, Zondervan (in association with the literary agency of Fedd & Company, Inc.), ©2011.

Other Great Resources Available at

www.tonysutherland.com

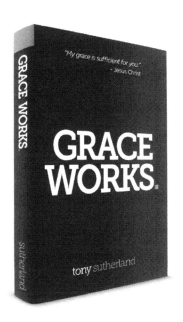